Beating the Odds

(A Story of the Odds Becoming a Stepping Stone of the Possibilities of Sophie's Life)

BASED ON TRUE EVENTS

PHYLLIS GOLDSBY

PAGE PUBLISHING, INC.
New York, NY

First originally published by Page Publishing, Inc. 2019

ISBN 978-1-64462-182-0 (Paperback)
ISBN 978-1-64462-183-7 (Digital)

Printed in the United States of America

Special Acknowledgements

M Y BIGGEST INFLUENCES IN WRITING this book and where my inspiration came from is God; my three children: Milan, Shayla, and Terrance. Special acknowledgement for someone who encourages me in life. May you rest in peace. You may be gone, but you are not forgotten. Your kindness and inspiration reign always in my heart and spirit: Great-Great Auntie Mag, Great-Great Auntie Alberta, and Uncle Kenny.

Introduction

T HIS BOOK IS ABOUT A young girl and the struggles she
had to go through as a child. It tells about her path of life all the
way up to becoming a woman. Sometimes, you have the know
the history to understand the present. In order to understand someone, you cannot go by what you hear. You have to get to know them
yourself. Sophie wants to tell her story, so you will get to know her.

"And Jesus looking upon them, saith, With men it is impossible, But not with God: for with God all things are possible."

—St. Mark 10:27

CHAPTER

1

M Y NAME IS SOPHIE, AND I have a story to tell about my will to survive. There are so many Sophies that look and appear to have the best upbringing. Sophie always thought whenever she assumed something, it would backfire. Most of the time, the only one that had Sophie's back was God. These days, more and more people are becoming unbelievers of God, for whatever may have happened to them in life or whatever reason. Sophie is not perfect, but she held on to the Almighty God that she knew when she was not even sure who she was. I am not writing to talk about anyone. I want to come forward and tell my story, and hopefully, it will inspire others, which I have always wanted to write a book, but about real-life situations, but not about me. I decided to write this book because there are so many people going through situations. People like myself that have helped so many people and lives and really need a caring hand themselves. I was so afraid to tell my story at this point in life. After I write this book, maybe I don't have to worry about people judging at work. Maybe this book will assist me in living financially and assisting people in living in their lives.

My story begins when I was born. I am the oldest of six children. I have three brothers and two sisters. Four of us are from New York, New York, and my sisters were born in Oakland, California. My mother is a native of Oakland, but her parents died when she was at a young age and was brought to New York to be raised by her great-aunt and uncle. My parents had us at a very young age. Mom was seventeen years old, and Dad was eighteen. My parents are so smart, but yet being young parents sometimes, school has to be placed on the back burner. My parents separated, and at the time of separating, I was too young to remember us ever living together as a family. When I went to school in New York, I was an average student because I thought it was cool to sit in the back of the class putting my feet on the chair. Most of the time, I lived with my great great aunt and my Uncle got hooked on heroin. It was very sad to see him nodding. My mom taught me to say my prayers, and I can say my mom was tough on me. I can truly say the best thing she ever taught me was to get down on my knees and say my prayers for my family. I, Sophie, the oldest of six children said my prayers every night for Uncle Leon who was on the hardest drug that I knew of as a little girl. One day, my prayers were answered, and Uncle Leon and some of his friends sought treatment and were able to wing out heroin with methadone. My uncle died, and I knew he was gone too soon. Uncle Leon did not die from a drug overdose but from health complication. I was glad to tell Uncle Leon a few years before he passed away that every night as a little girl, I prayed for him to stop using the needle (heroin). I also told him as I became a young woman that I am glad he got himself together. I told him when I was in Oakland because Uncle Leon still lived in New York and thought about his birthday party that I was unable to attend to.

In a single-parent home, you risk a greater chance of not being successful. I do not agree with that statement. There are a lot of people that came from single-parent homes that are successful. My mother moved with my brothers and I to Oakland when I was ten years old. At that time, I was the only girl. My sister came along when I was fifteen years old. I always wanted a little sister then I finally got one. When I turned twenty, I got another little sister. When we moved to California, we had to live with a cousin who had twelve children living downstairs, and her mother and father living next door. At that time, there were four of us. When we moved in our own apartment, I was so happy, and I did not even have a bed to sleep in. The carpet was the most beautiful carpet I had ever seen. I was so happy to once again live in a house with just our family. In New York, my mom went to school and continued working in Oakland while getting her G.E.D. My mom did get her G.E.D. I remember once as a kid in New York, my mom and I were on the bus. I got off the bus and mom stay on to go to her school: instead of me going across the street to school, I went straight to my great-great aunt's house. Her house was so huge. Once I was on the tricycle, I accidently rolled off the porch bike and all. I do not remember how old I was, but I remember the next-door neighbor running to my aid and picking me up quickly off the ground. The house was so huge there was a reception area as you walked in. There was a bench made into the wall and a desk with telephone on it. It also had a pantry and two ways to enter upstairs; it was a time when cities were still building freeways and highways, so the city brought all the houses out on that one side of the street. My great-great aunt took the money and brought another house and never had a mortgage on it to my knowledge. As a child, we spent a lot of time living with Great-Great Aunt Rose. She played a very important role in my life. I looked at Great-Great Aunt Rose like my grandmother. My mother and uncle called her Mama because she raised them after their parents died. I always came back to New York to visit her. It was one of the saddest days in my life when she passed away. Since I am a native of New York, I spent my entire life running back and forth from Oakland Public Schools all the way up to high school. I graduated from all New York Public Schools.

Some of the things I love to do as a child prepared me for my journey in life. Sometimes, how you are as a child, the adulthood is a reflection. I know I had what you called an old soul. I remember one time I had just enough money to buy a pair of winter boots I really wanted when I lived in New York. I would not eat when my friends and I went shopping. We went to this nice restaurant, and after they ate they just walked out, and once we got outside, one of them said

I could have eaten. I would not have wanted to eat that way. They had money to pay for their meals, but I just did not. We were all in our early teen years. My full name is Sophia Dominque Blue. My nickname is Sophie

My name Sophie has been my nickname just as my real name Sophia. When I was younger, I love to sing, dance, and write back home to New York. You weren't a true New Yorker child if you did not like to sing, dance or step to the beats or act. When my mother moved us to Oakland, life was not like we knew it. Our family was gracious enough to allow us to live in the home for two years. The household was a lot stricter than what I was accustomed to. We could listen to music sometimes but could not dance or sing in front of the elders for religious reasons. We were not allowed to play cards, but there were so many children living in the same home. We had look out people to see when the elders were coming. I also had to adjust my speech quickly. I learned that doggone was unheard of for a nine-year-old girl to use. Every Sunday, we had to gather around the small kitchen table to say the Lord's Prayer. At that time, there were about fifteen children and pets living in the same home. There was never a day without food.

After dinner, I would help my cousin wash the dishes. We could never allow dishes to sit overnight or let a pot soak. Every dish was washed clean and put away. I volunteered to wash the lunch dishes. So when I got home from school, I would wash and dry the dishes by myself and help my cousin at night. I believed every journey in my past life kept me traveling to work on my goals. As I got older, I think that I steered off the course, matter of fact I am sure of it. I started to have my own family; three children, two girls and a boy. Still, I was holding on to my dreams. I never lost sight of them. I just didn't know when or if they would surface back up and they did! Every time I wanted to continue my journey, my children's father had no job and asked who was going to watch the children. I remember I was working two jobs, and my children's father ran up my phone bill to $550 and never paid me a dime on it from calling another woman. I learned how to drive late in life. One snowy night, my car was stuck in the middle of the parking lot, and my children's dad got mad at me because I asked him to help me get the car unstuck. I have been single for a long time, but I have been enjoying my freedom. Life was very grim being a single parent, especially when all children had the same father. People tried to commend me by saying at least all your children have the same father, but I found it in my book coming from me to be unacceptable. I've never been married just banking on his promises. I felt like if one can look at my past situation, at least all my children had the same baby daddy, or I was stupid three times. Most of the times, money was very low to no money at all. Still I kept going. My family surely thought that man would be the end of me, but I grew strong and parted ways with him. I even started being interested in dating again. As I write this book, I've learned that being single can be used as an opportunity.

While I was pregnant with my first child, I was working on a college degree. There were whispers among other college students that I would not be graduating because the due date of my first child would interfere with finishing out my term. One of the students came up to me and said I heard you were not graduating this year. My response was that's funny, but I never got that information, and I do plan on graduating in May. The same year I graduated, my daughter was born in January, and I went back to school in January. She was born January 4, and two weeks later, I went back to school. I had no car and didn't have one until about seven years later.

As a child, I always wanted a glitzy lifestyle not because it was glitzy, but it was what I wanted to do. As a child, I wanted to become an actress, and now I am taking acting lessons. I am taking acting lessons as a hobby. My thought was and still is as long as God allowed me to see another day, I have an opportunity to improve my life. There are some dreams that I always wanted to do, and they are all in the process. I spent my whole life encouraging and lifting other people up and caring more for others' well-being with no regard to my own well-being. I never forgot three conversations with three people; one was a stranger at a bus stop, and the other was a former coworker. The man at the bus stop said, "You look like you should be riding in a Cadillac." Another man a coworker once told me, "You give very good advice, you should start following your own." When I was a teen, one man told me that he bet I sat on the porch. I have always had to fight to live a presentable lifestyle. A big inspiration in my life I would say would be my uncle. My uncle passed away too soon. I never forget how he would encourage me and have me do different chores that later in life would help with my skills. I remember he would always say books and boys don't mix. It is funny that as I write this book, I am single. After being in a relationship that was abusive more mentally than physically, maybe it is okay for now I can follow my dreams without having to answer to anyone. When I was a child, I remember this saying from a movie, "Success is nothing unless you have someone to share it with." I have learned when the term negative people are used my view point. It is not so much *that the people are negative; it's that one have to get with the type of people that accepts them. When I was a teenager*, I wanted to have my own clothing shop. I decided to go to college for fashion merchandising and design merchandising. I tried to get in the business, but I was having such a hard time. Me trying to help people, I remember a young lady and I both worked in the same department store, and I told her about the management training program; she was a person of color too. She did not even know about the program; the department store interviewed us both, but they hired her, not me. I was not mad. I just kept working in retail, and I did get a position in another store as a manager trainee. I did not settle; I just kept trying. I am not in my twenties when writing this book, but I feel that youthful self of the past set the way for my present self. I learned that when you are behind on your utility bills, it would depend on who I was talking to. They can work out a plan better than you think. I believe a lot of my blessing came from God and the philosophy I have in life. I learned that when you go to work, you are supposed to give it all. My boss had and has my utmost respect. I also learned that sometimes, it is best to just listen and not all the time voice your opinion. Let's talk about some of my goals in life and what happened. The day as I write this book, I had a very tough day. I am going to get started. I just want to be happy and have a piece of mind. One thing I want to point out when you are trying is don't ever give up.

To me, there was no more you can make it try, but you can make it if you try harder. Goals are something that always inspired me to do better. When it seemed like something was hopeless, I kept an optimistic viewpoint. I even had to change the type of people I was around. Just because one changes their circle that does not mean the circle was full of people more of wasting their dreams than chasing them. There are good people that just were not good for me to be around. When I thought about some serious times that I needed, support I could of have used true *blue* friends. Staying positive in a not-so-positive atmosphere is a fight within itself. Today, someone asked me how do I make it with all the expenses I have. My life should have been much better than it is, but each day that God allows me to see another day, another day I have an opportunity to be better than I was the day before. I told the person who asked me that question that I have made less money than this. The job before I returned into the property managing business was a part-time sales job. I would bring home the grand total of $352 a week. I quickly learned that you cannot take a job interview at face value. Even at the interview, you should ask the interviewer what position you are applying for. I was so excited I was going to be interviewed for an assistant store manager, in which it was a part-time sale.

I only accepted that job because my unemployment was to be running out in one week, and I had not worked good or a full-time job since 2012. I worked the part-time like I would work a full-time position. Another job I had for only a few months quoted me one annual salary but was much lower than what was said. It seemed like it should be a law about stretching the truth to hire someone. The lie just does not stop there in the interview; it travels to the pockets and disappoints a family such as mine and put them in despair. I have and had to fight for everything I want and get.

There were times that I would say in my thoughts that I just get so tired of fighting for everything I wanted. To me, it was like being on stage I did not open up to a lot of people. I see a lot of bill boards about hungry Americans. When I was really starting off in life a younger me, I had this Scarlett O'Hara attitude from *Gone with the Wind.* One of the most powerful scenes to me in the movie *Gone with the Wind* as beautiful as Miss O'Hara was that she was looking motley and said she would never go hungry again. The same type of drive and determination was what I have always been a single mother, and I always wanted my children to have a better life than me. I did not believe in dropping my children off with anyone. When I was dropped off or someone would babysit me, it would be a nightmare most of time.

Some of the scariest time of my life as a child was when my mother was not around.

The only time it was not bad when she was gone was when she left me in the care of Great-Great Auntie Rose. I never forgot when I was twelve years old. My mom wanted to go out with her friend. Her friend's nephew lived with her. This nephew woke me up because I felt some heavy arms around me in the bed. As I recalled, he had moved his little cousins as they slept to the other twin bed, and he was in the bed with me. I believe that I woke up in time. I jumped out of the bed and told him I was telling my mother. He began to beg and offered me two dollars not to tell. I threw his money on the floor and told him in a grumpy little voice of a twelve year old, "I don't want your money!" I could not go to sleep for the rest of my stay. The next day, I hung in the kitchen with my mom not knowing how to tell her. I was so afraid, so I never did. I mentioned in college in a class I was in. I have had other cases like this as a child in the hands of a babysitter, and I was afraid to tell my mother. I believe that was sexual abuse there, and sexual abuse was done to me; there was no such thing as boys will be boys. I did a lot of going back and forth as a child living from New York to Oakland. I spent my entire life going back and forth, staying, visiting. One city I could go to back at night as a child, and I slept like a princess, and when going to another city, sleeping at night would be a struggle for there was an older boy who was jumping in my bed and another little one in the bed younger than me. I never forget one night, a boy jumped in my bed, and I was trembling so bad at that time. I believe I was ten years old. The bigger boy said, "You are shaking." It was such a nightmare to endure abuse where you stayed.

This boy would also hit a lot and even paid another boy to jump on me on the way back from the candy store. My life was tough by the age of thirteen (now as I write this part, I felt a slight headache because this is another hard part that I have learned to put behind me). I had a nervous breakdown at the age of thirteen years old. I could not speak; I was beginning not to recognize my own family. At the hospital, the staff members if they looked like someone in my family, before I lost my speech, I would say they were the family members. I remember getting a CAT scan, and I was so wild and could not speak. The person pinned my long pony tails to the cat scan table, so when I tried to get up, I could not. I had stopped eating my food. I was five feet seven inches, and I was a regular thirteen year old. I wore Junior Miss 5/6. When I had my breakdown, I wore a little girl's size 14 clothes. My mother told me when I got better that she thought I was going to die. Anyone that came to the apartment before I was hospitalized, I was crying so bad. My behavior was off the Richter scale with the tears. Finally, my mom realized that I was not kidding or being funny. Something had gone wrong in her daughter. Can't say for sure what triggered it, maybe it was from mistreatment or the abuse as a child.

When people looked at my resume, or I tell them my educational background, one would wonder why I barely have food in the refrigerator or how I could possibly be out of full-time employment for three years. Inside of me, I always felt that there was something else in life I should be doing. It just seems like all my aspirations and promising career were just a dream. I always learned or heard the term or phrase "you can make it if you try." It seems like I was giving great advice, but I was not following some of my own advice. I would tell someone how to handle a certain situation, and most of the time, they would be fine. If someone reads this book and say if she can make it regardless of what happened to her, surely, I can make it. If ever I was interviewed, a good question would be to ask me what makes me persevere, I would have to say to have the ability to help when and where I can. I know God has an Angel watching me. I have not worked on this book in several days. It seems like I want to attempt to work on this book when I am extremely sleepy or extremely tired. At this very moment, I want you to know I should be in the bed because it is 2:05 a.m., and I have to get up for work. I want to focus now; no matter what I have been through, it makes me the person who I am. What I learned in life sometimes, some people tend to judge me on what they perceived me to be. When I was growing up, I wanted to go to college because I thought that it would be my ticket to never being hungry, never wanting or needing anything, and never being broke. To me, it was becoming more of a pipe dream with disappointments. God never let me give up on my dreams. I am not even sure that everything that I put in this book should even be in this book. I just want to let people know that every situation that you may go through does not have to be permanent. No one knows what secrets a person had been carrying through the years or what type of situation one may have been in. Sometimes, people tend to be the most critical without looking at the bigger picture.

I have tried so many times at doing some things to be success-ful. Sometimes, it takes me years to accomplish my goals. I never give up on what I want to do. I understand that writing an interesting book is important. I hope this book will motivate someone to do what they want to do despite the odds. The first piece of advice is to get my priorities straight. I had dreams and still have dreams. So I have to be motivated when success seems so far for me. Some days, I would just be complacent with what I had and thought to myself this is as good as it's going to get me. There are other days when I say to myself as long as God allows me to see another day, I need to make it count. Some days I felt like I was not amp up enough or thirsty enough to do all the things I want to do, at least most of them. I also learned that success does not lie in how much money I made, it lied in how I made a change in my life for the better. I know people who rather stay at home until they can find the job they are looking for. You see I would take a job to keep myself afloat. There is nothing wrong with staying with a job until you find the one that you really want. Our goals and dreams are good to have.

Bringing one's dream to reality takes a lot of work. I have an appointment book I use a lot. Now this book has become a goal.

There is one person in this book that seemed interested in how my book is coming along. How should I write this book? Today, I am thinking now that I got some shocking truth out. I think I may write it as a dairy. I can understand why writers struggle with writing block. It just what it is, writer's block. It is like you want to write, but the enthusiasm isn't there.

Today, I thought I should have motivated myself more than I do. I do great work when I am employed. I even put in so many hours knowing I will not get paid for it. Employers can fire you no matter how hard you work. Some states have a fire-at-will law. This tells me you can have the best work and one of the most hardworking workers there is, but you can still be let go. I was listening on the radio the other day, and the DJ asked this question when is it time to reach on your goals. I was driving, but I should have not have gotten out the car unless I heard the answer. In my mind, I knew the answer, whether or not the answer was a match.

It is my belief that you should never give up on your hopes and dreams as long as you are able to go out there and chase the dreams and goals and turn them into reality.

People tend to either judge me or try to put me down. I was thinking to myself what could possibly be so fascinating about me that a lot of people that I want to befriend act like they do not want to associate. Yes, I am pretty; yes, I work hard; and yes, I am kind, so why wouldn't everyone that comes in contact with me want to be my friend? Are they negative people? My answer would be no. My mom had given me the best advice that I could have as a child; not everyone will like you. All throughout, school girls would start fights with me. I was so humble, but looking back, I was young, pretty and smart, and all I ever wanted was to be accepted for being me. Bouncing from one state to another with my mom and siblings did not make it any easier as far as fitting in. I never was part of the crowd, and I never wanted to hang within crowd. These days and times, the world is so on its ears.

CHAPTER

2

I T IS ALWAYS GOOD TO be yourself because the right people for you will come and embrace them, make them feel like they are appreciated. To me, it is better to be around people that you get along with instead of people that you have to deal with. I learned that life can throw you a curve ball. I do a lot of praying and believing that God will make a way. When one wants to be successful in life, no matter how long it takes, just do it. I must say to myself how it is that there are situations that are such a mess. I can come in and sort it out. The secret is a lot of hard work.

In order to achieve anything in life, a lot of work have to be put into it. If someone receive something that they did not work for at all, then the bottom line is, one will have to work to keep it. I myself had to start from scratch. One thing to remember is not to let your dreams and goals go no matter how far away they may seem.

I can be honest and say I almost let my dreams and hopes and goals ride away in the sunset. My life was nothing like I picture it to be. Let me share what I thought my life was going to be like. I am actually amazed that people just presume that I was on top of the world, when inside my soul and spirits felt like they were climbing out of a muddy hole for years looking back every now and then. I never felt sorry for myself. Again, I just cannot believe that I am seriously writing a book. This book was definitely not in my plans, but God must want me to get this book written. I am going to put a greater effort in this book. Tonight, I did not do badly. If I can be motivated and not fall off the wagon of success, then the book will be completed this year. I spoke to someone of how hard it is to want to write a book, but sometimes, I am not in the mood. Now for example, I am starting to get a little sleepy. I am going to type a little more and get some shut-eye.

I hope my sentence prior to this one was inspiring. Being sleepy and still typing shows how bad I want my book to be published. As I type this part, I am on page 10.

I said when I write this book, I need to write as the mood sets the tone. Please forgive me if I jumped around in this book. I've never been well in English, but I love to chat.

Hmmm, I think I talked a little bit about my love life. My love life has not been that great at all. As a matter of fact, it has been terrible. I always wanted to marry and stay married, but it has not happened. This message as I typed this part about not having any good relationships, I am feeling a little stronger. I want to say to everyone who has not dated in a while to keep doing your thing if it is positive and productive. I do not know why I have not met the right man yet. Chasing someone does not work for me because sooner or later, the love of the man's eye will pop up, and then I will end up hurt and embarrassed. When I did not have children, it would be the same thing wanting my dream man to come on a white horse like a knight in a shining armor. I would not want for anything, and he would make it clear that I am it for him. My true love I thought was with my children's father, but after I have taken mental cruelty from him, we decided to part ways but remained friends. This is another message to send out, my friends and I always thought that we could do badly by ourselves. When you really want some things for yourself, you can do better without people who are making your life not so good. Even though I am single, I am using this time to live my life and do the things I want to do. I am learning how to play the piano, involve in acting lessons, and join in real estate. It does not pay to be intimidated about your future. In my life, I was intimidated by my own motivation.

Once when I was starting college, I felt afraid of what was ahead. I know I wanted to be successful, but I was afraid. I did graduate from college, and I did get over the fear. I then needed to allow my college degree to work for me. The second one was getting my real estate license. Sometimes, I do not have the motivation for myself to get this book done. I know I should get the book done. I believe that people should really know that even though the grass may look greener, on the other side it isn't.

I have never been a competitive person and never could understand that some people does not know how to accept kindness. Again, this book is about motivation and some of the difficult times I had in my life. I read so many self-help books and seen and listened to motivational speakers. My life is far from perfect, but I learned it is worth letting people know that I just want to be myself, and it's okay to be yourself. Being in the hospital for a few months from a nervous breakdown at the age of thirteen years old is not the only time I was hospitalized, and at a very young age as a child, I had the illness called scarlet fever. When I lived in New York, I got the scarlet fever.

I am not for sure how old I was when I had the illness scarlet fever, but I do know I was younger than eight years old, and it was very difficult for me. I know I was sitting in the floor, but my skin was discolored down to my feet; and the next thing I could remember, I was in the hospital for weeks. Every time I see my family, I wanted to come home. I know I was in the hospital for several weeks. I am very grateful that the rest of my siblings did not catch it. I have kept so many do not talk a lot about my hard times because I was told not to, because people will treat you differently. If people hear, that you had a nervous condition before, they may treat you like cannot function and work just as well as people who have not. I have been told it will judge and label you as crazy. I feel like it happened to someone else because it felt after the healing that the nightmare happened to someone else. I believe that as a child, I just could not continue to handle the stress that I had endured and did not have anyone that had taken the time out to really know me, and I was afraid that it would be repercussion because as a child, I had no protection in what would happen if I said anything. As I got older, I realized I was doing a lot better than some of the people I would run into on the streets that I knew had mental illnesses too. I looked at it this way. People have to understand more of what the illness is about. To me, upon writing this book, I feel like I am coming out of the closet in rare form. Yes, I have been mistreated, misjudged and ill, and I've been through it all. I got down on my knees and prayed to God like I always have done. I know some people do not believe in God. I believe in him, and if a person treated me right no matter what that person believed, it was not for me to judge. I was not sure if I will write another book because I had no clue I would be writing a book. I wonder how it will sell. Guess what? God willing, in two weeks, on November 13, is my birthday.

It would be nice if I had a date to go out and talk and have a great meal with someone who I think has a beautiful personality inside and out, but it does not look that way. I ask God to send me someone that has his approval. I also want to say this to anyone who wants to be in a serious relationship (I went to hear an author speak on relationships). The author went on to say that if you are single, you will meet the right person for you. The saying that there is someone for everyone just may hold some truth!

I just want more than dating. At this time in my life, the next man I date must be real with me and dates only me. My children's father is eight years older than me. Now I am realizing that age is not always the issue at hand. I have met some very mature men that who are younger than I. However, I have lost count as of the years that I have not been on a date or even in a loving conversation. I know one day, I will meet someone who knows how to return the love I am giving them and ask for my hand in marriage. I hope that my readers of my book, if you have not found true love, do not give up because someone may be searching for you at this very moment.

When I was a child, I always spent time searching for happiness. For a long time, I felt that I was robbed and cheated out of my childhood, and I have always love people and believed and treating them properly. I always want to make a difference in someone's life. I always like my children to have a better life. I read in a book that if a person does not treat you right, they will not treat your children right. Everyone's not born into this so-called good life. Life is only what you can make. You can be born into happiness and can lose it too. Every day is not going to be a good day, but my philosophy of life is if you dream it, you can live it, be it or make it, if the goal is possible.

Each day I wake up is a chance I can be a better person than I was the day before. I am not into insulting other people. I'm not into competing with other women because I am too busy competing with myself. I found that I am too busy trying to pull myself to another level. I just maybe able to help another person. I have too many tough times in my life including utilities being shut off, eviction notices too, and sometimes no food.

As I write this book, all my utilities are on, all the eviction notices I got for my home, I now own. As I write this book, my refrigerator is so packed with food. I really should invest in a freezer. As I drive home from work, it feels so good that I cannot make up my mind on what to make instead of going home to some canned goods that came from the free-food place. I always do my best to stay humble. My past suffering reminded me to be humble. I remember when I was a child, my mother taught me to never refuse what's on the plate that is given to me even if I do not like it. I remember as children, by the end of the month, we had no food. My mother taught me even if I am hungry that when offered with food, I should always say no thank you. When the neighbors and I would be talking what we had for dinner, sometimes I would make up these elaborate dinners (laughing but sad); in fact, I may not even eaten a piece of bread.

My children laughed about what I am about to say as if it is unbelievable. At this time, I still was the oldest of four children; the only item in the house was a potato, so my mom gave that baked potato to my youngest baby brother who really was a baby. There was ketchup in the house, so I ate the ketchup. I'm saying this to say that all that I have been through in life, I still pray, and I believe in a miracle every day, and that God will make a way out of no way. I believe that faith in God can keep and have kept me in motivational state. Let me reveal the motivational quote that I saw on my social media account.

Motivational quote: "Be happy with the little that you have. There are people with nothing that still managed to smile" (Motivation for Life @ MotivatedLiving). The last time I put an entry in this book was January 25, 2016. I must finish this book because once finished, I would like to do a book of poems dedicate to all the women.

Being a woman myself I know I have struggled with a lot of things. My social life has not been that great, but I tried really hard. Sometimes when I try too hard, people think that I am a Miss Goody Two Shoes, which is what I have been called as a child. I've never seen myself as a Miss Goody Two shoes and certainly never thought I was better than anyone. I have known what I wanted to be happy in life and wanted people to accept me for my personality and not to judge me for my personality. Trust is a big deal to me because people have taken my kindness for weakness, and for the hard lesson I am taught in life, it was hard for me to trust. I started to realize that no matter how hard I try to, everyone is not going to like, and as a matter of fact, in some cases, one may not be liked because you tried so hard. I learned that there will be those that will accept you, and there will be those that will not. The lesson I learned is that my struggle is real, but I have to keep moving. I should be almost done with the book. It's now March and need to finish it up. When obstacles get in your way, you must keep your eyes on the prize and keep it until you can see progress. I have learned that the saying is so true that you can make it if you try or try harder.

To me, it's so sad when a person is mean to someone for no reason. There could be just so much more to be done with all the talents and precious gifts that had been bestowed upon us. It is never too late to start a journey when God has given me a chance to get some rest and be ready to continue on.

My parents basically told me to be careful what I write. I want this book to be about a little girl to a woman who always sought to be herself and only imagine that life can be so much more than what it is and what it was and not let anyone try to tear her down. People will try to tear you down without even giving you the opportunity to give you the chance to even get to know the real you. I have been blessed that every job I have done rather it be work for pay or work for free I always put my 110 percent in it.

I have not finished this book but already have an idea to what the next book will be like. It has always been hard for me to hold a job. I always do the best I can, but some states have the right to fire at will. I always thought in my mind that I have always done well at work. From my experience in all my jobs, I have found out what the issues were, and I assisted to correct them. There is also the EEOC that one can go to see if the firing was justifiable sometimes. They may see your point according to the rules and guidelines, and sometimes, they may not see your point according to the rules and guidelines. What I have learned in the workforce is never tell them that you are looking for another job and never tell your personal business at work even on your worst days. Sometimes, after you sort out the mess, you were hired to clean up. There are people that all of a sudden, they want your job, or you may be pushed out. I look at it as an opportunity to do something else. Maybe what I was doing in the first place was not my calling. If I get successful to do something else well, I was truly sent on my way to a better way to help someone else. Sometimes, you may feel that you are getting the short end of the stick, but that is quite alright. You just keep trying, and it will be alright. A perfect example was I got lost during the earlier part of this week. I am a west-sider, but I had to take a poll worker class on the deep eastern beautiful suburb when I got lost. I was doing well I got to the roundabout in the road. I had to go to the roundabout at least three times raining heavily. I called the library twice once for directions and the other to let the poll worker teacher know I was lost and just could not make it. The librarian informed me that she could not give that message. Miraculously as I continued to drive, I stumbled upon the library. I thought I would be turned away because

I was late, but instead, when I arrived, the classroom was filled. The teacher was polite, and the class started laughing, probably looking buck-eyed that I made it when I told them I got lost. Never give up too soon. You do not know how close you truly are. What inspires you against the odds?

I always thought of myself of really doing something with my life. I always like to help people. Maybe because of the plight of my own life I do not know. I know what it's like not to have the finances to do what I really like to do. For example, for a couple of years I was unemployed, I did receive unemployment, but I still have bills out there that needed quick attention. I got no food stamps.

In some of the free-food places, the food would make my stomach hurt, so I really had to be careful where I went. My water was turned off twice; that was a nightmare. As I write this book, I can say that my water and sewer bill is at a zero balance until I get my next bill. Being hungry is not a good thing. Food is so important to have, and when you don't have the resources to get food, you should not eat something that makes your tummy hurt, so I stopped going to that particular free-food place. When I lost my job, I experienced flood in my home, and the insurance company would not touch it with a ten-foot pole; matter of fact, they dropped me. I lost my job, and I had to take out a loan against the house, which is something I hope I do not have to do again. I was grateful and felt blessed that the city assisted in making repairs to the home, and I got into a program where my property taxes and my equity loan to make repairs were paid off by the government. I needed the loan for new windows, carpet and plumbing. I did not even expect the windows and carpet.

What I learned is you should do something for your home at least once month no matter how small or large it may be. I hope I never have to take out another loan against the house. To me, it seems too risky. If one defaults, you could lose your home. If you just have to take out a loan because things do happen, pay the loan back and communicate with the loan agency if you are in a jam. There are so many options out here that may have qualified one for assistance. Education have been an important part of life. Being a single parent is a struggle, but nowadays, raising children in a two-parent household is a challenge too. At one point, a friend of mind asked me about my parenting even though she was married. My family is not perfect by a long shot. As I write this book, my oldest daughter graduated from college two years ago, and my baby girl will be graduating from college this year. My son will finish his requirements this year to receive a high school diploma. I am not a grand mama yet, but I hope my kids will be prepared. When I raise my children, I wanted them to have a better upbringing than I had. When they do decide to have children God willing, Grandmama will be there for them. Happiness is not a genie in a bottle.

I remember talking to a relative over the phone and saying I just want to be happy. My relative basically told me that happiness is not 24 24 emotions. I have learned in life that happiness is making others happy. Sometimes, I have learned that it's okay to do things to make you happy. It is okay to have a me day or my time. Once my children became young adults, I was still rushing home, but I found them to not be there and doing their own thing. Still I come home like I still have three little children to rush to get from the day care. I started going out again, but by myself. I went to see a world-renowned pianist, a comedian and play and a few movies alone. Sometimes, you just got to get out there by yourself or stay at home by yourself. What's that famous phase we must do lunch, but it never happens, now I would like to do something at least once a month. I believe that life is only what you make it. Some will approve of you, and some will not. Get with those that want to be around you. I learned never to hang around long to prove a point because you refuse not to be ran out of anywhere. Staying where you are unhappy leaves you with no room for growth and for you to truly be yourself, so I decided to live my life and ask for guidance and grace and mercy from God.

If I had not let, go and let God I probably would not be writing this book right now. Sometimes, one can get all hung up on trying to please the wrong people. It can exhaust one, and no energy is left for you to do your thing. Focus and staying focused is very difficult when there are so many other distractions. With talking about my life and goals in this book, I ran into some distraction. To be honest, I have too much unfinished things to do. Some days I felt like I do not have the stamina to finish this book. I wonder if it is because I don't have a mate to push me on or because there are days that I am just mentally strained and just have enough strength to do what I needed to do and come home. Life is only what you make it People often ask why I do not have a husband or boyfriend. I supposed one has to go out to meet people, and when I do go out, it's a play house, movie, and orchestra hall, places like that. I hope God have picked a man especially for me. I do not know when this mystery man will come into my world, but I will be already. Already be ready forever.

Being ready is an important part of life. Always have a couple of black dresses in your closet; men always have a couple of suits in their closet. You do not always have to have something new to wear for an occasion; it always feels great that you always make sure that you keep your clothes clean whether you take them to the cleaners or wash them. It's nothing like saying let me go to my closet to pull something out to wear because someone just asked me to show up at an important event. Already be ready so you will not worry about getting something done at the last minute, and it's close, or you are inconveniencing someone else, but they do it anyway. I speak from experience. As I am typing, I just hope that I can talk about myself for one hundred pages. I have always tried to be humble and courteous to others; sometimes, your kindness may rub off on another person. I remember watching television, and just when I was turning the TV channels, I saw this man on television talking. When my home was flooding, I e-mailed him talking about different things. Once I met him, and I never thought I would. We follow each other on some social media, but my point is, I saw him on TV and never thought I would meet him, and we hugged. I am saying this to say the impossible can become the possible. When I met him, we probably were on different planes. He was around a crowd of people, and to me, it was a moment for life, and I never saw him again except on social media, but again, the impossible can become the possible. It is good to meet people and enjoy meeting people. As I am typing, the impossible is going through my head. What if this book really sells?

This can be possible. It is possible for me to finish this book. I started on this book toward the end of last year, and I must work on it as much as possible even if it is only for ten minutes, at least I got some work in. I would like to move to another state. Sometimes, I believe that I am single because maybe I need to have more freedom to do whatever is necessary for me to do where there is no need to say stop they are taking advantage of you or see what I mean.

Some days, it does get lonely. I would not be human if some-times I did not get lonely. I just need to finish the rest of things I have started in this book. The more I type, the quicker I will be finished. Some such as myself people are meant to do certain things before I had decided to write a book. I always felt that there was something like a part of me I really need to do. Rather or not it is the writing of this book and putting out another one I do not know. I think having dreams are so beautiful, and when they come to life, it becomes even greater. A dream that coming to life is larger than life. The time I am writing this book, the United States have their first black president, but this recent election, that will happen, seems to have most on edge. I mean this is the first time I did not know who to vote for in the primary, but still, I wanted my vote to count. There are many ways to vote, and I do not understand why some people feel that their vote do not count.

If everyone felt that their vote does not count, and no one voted, what would happen?

I have worked the voting polls this primary, and it took hours, but it was educational and rewarding. Both times I worked at the polls, and I have met public figures who have helped people. Both were very conversational. One even took a picture with another fellow voter. You also get paid for helping at the polls, but to me, the money is not as important as the experience. Being kind to others is so much easier than being unkind.

Some folks think that being mean at work is the key to success. What drives me is perseverance and getting the job done. When I was young, I was working at a fast food restaurant, and the manager was training us for work; and to me, at the time, I was about eighteen years of age. Two things I remember her telling the staff before I started working was there would be no gossip; and if we have time to lean, we have time to clean. I did not have a car, so she would give the young people a ride home. If she knew I was writing a book and all the struggles that I had in life since she met me, I believe she would not feel sorry for me but would talk with me and not criticize me and be very proud of me that I kept pushing despite the odds. When you want to make a change in your life, you can make it if you try harder. I'm just thinking, will I meet the man of my dreams while I am writing this book, or will I meet him later? I want to be in love again, but I know if you love and the love is not being returned, it is a terrible feeling. I just want the world to know that life is for the living and do not let the world pass you. There are so many opportunities in life; we just have to be willing to take them. Being too hard on yourself is not a good thing at all, but showing discipline for yourself is very good. It's good to get out and enjoy yourself sometimes, even if the money is tight.

I tried to keep myself busy, and something I am trying is to do something at least once a month. I find it to be the most rewarding. Going out to lunch and dinner with someone once a month isn't bad. I noticed that these all you can eat restaurants, some of them are pulling at all the stops. Recently, I had lunch with a high school friend, and it was good to talk with someone who has known me for years. It was funny because we both did not eat at all that day. When we arrived at the restaurant, it was 4:00 p.m. The food was so good and worth the wait. One thing that I do not understand is when I hear people say basically at a certain age that dreaming is over. To me, most reality starts as a dream.

If you are still able to get out and about and have a vision, why not go for it? I know finances may be a hold up sometimes. I remember I would think to myself if I made a lot of money, what I would do to help others who just really could not help themselves. I believed in helping others who are in need. What I do find unacceptable is people using others, and once they cannot use them no more, they throw their friendship out the window. I think trying hard has made me a stronger person. One would think that to learn in life, everyone around me does not mean that everyone around they want to see me succeed. Of course, there are people out there who are just thinking about themselves. I have heard people say I got mine now, you got to get yours, or nobody helped me. I had to get it on my own, so the handwriting on the wall you got to get yours on your own. I have heard some sad clichés. One of the saddest clichés I heard is people who are on public assistance would have more babies to get more aid. To me, that's like the babies have to be taken care of, and public assistance is not giving out money like that, at least I do not think so. I know, unfortunately, I never married my children's father. They all have the same father. I was forced to received public assistance, even though most of the time I work. I never said I am not going to work but stay home and collect a welfare check. I do not even like using that term welfare. When I was not working, it's because I did not have a choice. When I was trying to work, the doctor said that my firstborn was a little underweight, so at that point, I had to let my manager job in a shoe store go. I had all kinds of crazy hours, and I really depended on my children's father to assist me, but it was amazing what happened. Women I did not even know were coming to me aggressively saying that they were taking care of my firstborn. So to receive a welfare check of $273 a month is hardly a luxury that I would stop working. I could never understand how I would stand in those public assistance lines and try to get emergency help, and the man in front of me got help while I myself with a baby in the stroller could not get help. As a little time went on, my daughter's godmother said why you don't try to get food stamps? At that point, I just went and applied. I never stayed in the program too long. I always believed that public assistance for me was just a temporary thing in my current but temporary situation. Even though people have said to me that I have such a beautiful personality, to me, I was just being myself even on my darkest days. I am grateful because I believe that one day, everything will get better. Most importantly, I always give thanks to God. I know he was there with me during my tough times. I believe in God and proud to say it. So much has happened in my life, and I prayed, and my prayers have been answered. Even though I am still single, my life is so full and getting fuller. I think writing this book is good for my spirit and soul. I have had so many let downs and disappointments in life, which is what drives me to drive harder. Sometimes, I think that some of the jobs I have been through was not meant for me to be comfortable and to continue to do what I should be doing or started doing. Some people are afraid of other people who are walking in and out of their lives like a revolving door. I know it is a terrible feeling, but each time someone walks in and out of my life, when I really think about that person, was not very kind. For a long time, it was hard for me to trust someone, and as crazy as it sounds, I was better striking up a conversation with a stranger. I did not have to worry about hearing it again. One of my daughters told me that she wished she could be like me who's able to strike up a conversation with anyone. My mom called it a gift of gab. Being able to strike up a conversation with anyone has its ups and down.

CHAPTER

3

I HAVE LEARNED SOME THINGS IN life. For example, if one does not want anyone to know their deepest darkest secrets, do not tell a soul. If you do not tell a soul, you do not have to worry about it getting out. For example, do not tell anyone at work you are looking for another job even if it is your work buddy because they will tell. Sometimes, they do it to save their own jobs or to see you get in trouble. Once I was working part-time, I thought I was being interviewed for a full-time managerial job but come to find out it was part-time. My unemployment was about to run out, so I took the job. I did my best to look my best and was very kind to everyone. Come to find out the person that told me to come in for the interview, it was his position that I was applying for not knowing he had already gotten the job. It is said that men make more money than women, and it had been proven time and time again. Sometimes, I know that I should be making more money than I have been making, but I do not fault anyone. Sometimes, it could be the opportunities that are presented to you; and sometimes, there are setbacks. I hear this motivational phrase on the radio a lot: "A setback is a setup for a comeback!" When I heard this, it was such an inspiration. Sometimes, you have to learn from your past; let your past be your guide to your future. I remember as a child I lived in two different environments; it was like the tale of two cites. One city my environment was where a laundry person picked up the household bedding, brought them back folded and pressed. A housekeeper showed me how to tie my shoes, but my great-great aunt was not rich; she just managed her money. The other tale was when we moved to another city, we ate very late. My mother bought a coat from the goodwill that cost .25, and the tag with the safety pin was still on it. I remember that coat so well it had a hood on it, and it fitted just perfectly for me.

I remember not having any winter boots to wear to school. I would wear my cloth tennis shoes. I remember there were a whole bunch of old shoes in my relative hall closet. To me, it was like the ones own personal goodwill. There were so many children in the house. With me and my siblings, it was about maybe at least fifteen children. Well, I put on these old boots that my cousin no longer could wear, or they were fashionably outdated. The boots were too big, but I was running late for school, and I put on those too large boots and my twenty-five-cent coat and off I went. Sometimes, our clothes were too big or really out-dated, and our relatives that we lived with laughed at us, but to me, it was truly sad. Today, the good-will clothes are much more fashionable. Recently, I brought some beautiful coats from there. For a long time, I would not buy used clothing. A used clothing store is a great place to shop, but the items needed to look right on you, but that is anywhere. It's so funny that all my life I love the world of fashion. Sometimes, if you do not have the right clothing and you like fashion on the outside, looking in it is really pleasing. I could say that to make it and I had the money, I would really look sharp. One of my degrees from college is in fashion merchandising, and I also went to a fashion college. Money was tight, but I made it through. I have also done some modeling. When a modeling agency came, to Oakland, I was chosen. I had also been chosen to compete with other models in New York. I do not think I regret not taking these opportunities because education was so important to me, and not to mention the amount of money that was needed to get myself the commercial training and more pictures. If

I had the money, I probably would have at least gotten the training. I had already struggled to get through one modeling training session and pictures from another agency. To me, $800 is a bit much especially when making a minimum wage at that time. Recently, I burned my wrist area and part of my arm due to a cooking accident. I put ice on my arm, and it eased the burn. I put Vaseline on it, and it started burning really bad. I was hungry, so right after I came home from working at the voting site I started cooking. I have been taking care of these burn marks on my arm. Working at the voting polls is very interesting as this is also an interesting political time. I have been working at the voting polls for two years. Every year, I meet a public figure when I work at the voting site. Even though being a poll worker has long hours, its experience is great.

It is like you are very much dependent upon when you work at the polls. To me, the money can always come in handy. When you can help someone, it is a good thing. People have to also learn to help themselves. Sometimes after being down for so long, it often seems like nothing is going to change. You have been dreaming for so long that people started to lose faith, in your dreams. Sometimes, when I feel that way, I keep on pushing. I had to ask myself why every time I keep pursuing something like the same thing, it constantly blows up in my face, or I found myself working two jobs trying to support my family. When my children were younger, I never called off work. I needed a job, and I wanted to save my sick time for if my children got sick. Folks would say to me I just come to work sick. I had gotten too ill, and for a whole year, I was misdiagnosed to find I had asthma. Life is too short. Before all this had happened, I remembered the day I got ill. I had an allergic reaction, and I was trying to calm the burning down on my skin with a cool cloth, but it had gotten worse. I never had this problem in life. A friend said that someone have done something. My children were still small, and I had one long phone cord that stretched through the house. I got ill in the front part of the house, and the phone was in the back part. It was about a week or so before Christmas, the tree was up, and the gifts were wrapped. When I spoke to the person on the phone, I was so weak I could not even make it back to the front part of the house. The emergency person was so kind, but he asked me to look to see what color my hands were, and I saw they were starting to turn blue. I do not know how I was still able to be coherent. I told my oldest daughter to open up all the outside doors of the house. My daughter said there were two ambulance trucks out there. I thank God I was pulling through. Once I was so ill, I was in my twenties, and I started throwing up a lot, and I went to the doctor, and I was told that I was in a high level of the illness, but I would need a surgery. God was watching over me. Sometimes, when I would walk, I would feel like the weight of the world was on my shoulders, and I did not have children. My three children are a blessing to me.

I know God has brought me through so much. Because of my blood type after my first child, my doctor told me if I did not get a shot at a certain stage of my pregnancy, my last two children may not have made it past two years old. God was watching over them and me. Two of my children graduated from college, and one is an aspiring inventor and aspiring rapper. We must always encourage our children and our young people and older people of their dreams. Sometimes we put our dreams on hold and may have to do what they have to do in order to survive. I was sick for one week. Today is the first day that I felt better. I still went to work. I had once read in a book that it is best to go to the emergency room with your children than to miss work; another option was to miss work at least as possible. I went to work programs too. For a while, I would not have accepted any public assistance, but I was not making enough money; and one time I had no work and needed food for my children. A dreamer never gives up on dreams. An entrepreneur can be made of almost anything. Sometimes, you have to be creative. Once I heard about a person charging to just stand in line for people. Standing in line for people can be a business I thought that was very smart. These days, it's good to think of a business plan if one is interested in entrepreneurship. I think if there are lot of opportunities a city has to offer and you are on public assistance it should be used as a stepping stone, and not a way of life, they can do better. It's funny looking for a job these days if you do not even have to go outside your home. It is good to get out when one is not working. When I was looking for work when the children were still small, I would take them to school, and then I would be dressed up and go to a job finding office; those places are awesome. You could sign up for various courses they had to offer. I think they would even send out your resumes to the place where you want them to go. The last time I wrote something in this book is about a week ago. The Sunday before last, I felt so good. I went out and brought me a very large milk shake with the cookies in it. That was the same day I was cooking dinner and all of a sudden, I could barely make it from the kitchen to the living room though it's very close. I almost just fell over sideways.

I love animals, but I felt like I was an animal about to keel over sideways. I thought to myself why would God allow this kind of deadly situation happen to me, or could I have been food poisoned from milkshake? I thought there are so many corrupt people in the world. What did I do to be struck like that? I then came to my senses, my thoughts, then I thought I am a human being. Humans are not perfect, and we get sick sometimes. This is not God's fault, but I do believe he kept me from falling over and had me able to finish my cooking. I had a headache and then I had vomited during that same week. I vomited at work. I probably should not have been trying to work, but I wound up going home from work early. I could not make it to the bathroom, so I wound up throwing up in a trash can that was lined. I went to a health fair at the end of the week, and my blood pressure went up a little high. I had been going to the gym but slacked up. I have started to do exercise at home. I will start back by going to a type of group exercise again. There are recreational centers that offer free exercise programs. I know I have a lot on my plate the last time I went to the doctor. My blood pressure was fine. I went to check my blood pressure in a local pharmacy. It went up one more notch, it was the hypertension area. I am going to check it again. My headache did go away, and I hope my blood pressure went down to where it usually be. If my blood pressure is not back down to normal, I have to go to the doctor. My parents are not in the best of health, and at this point, my mother needed twenty-four hours care. Deadlines that I had to meet and not going to bed earlier and getting up early may have all contributed to my blood pressure going up a bit. This is not the first time that this had happened. I did not have to take medicine for it. I changed the way I was doing things. Some things may not be fixed like changing the way one does things. I had the strangest dream.

A pastor I've known for years in a sermon stated to pay attention to your dreams. About a month ago, I dreamed about beautiful birds that came to my window, and I was feeding them, and all of a sudden, a very large bird, it was a palanquin, took the food from the two smaller birds. It was strange because the two smaller birds were beautiful fuchsia tones. I know I had a crush on two men. I was always hoping that one of them would step up and show interest in me enough to want to date me. They never did. So I wondered if the dream meant that those two handsome hardworking men did not need or deserve my kindness. I did not know the meaning or maybe the dream meant nothing. It is funny sometimes I will stay somewhere just because I was taught at a young age in New York never to run from your problems. My friend's mother said that once you start running, you will continue to run the rest of your life. When I told one of my brothers that I was going to write a book, he said in a text he wanted to know if it was going to be a mommy dearest and then a LOL (laugh out loud) in the end. My response, back in a text, was basically this book is to encourage others. I know it is hard being a single parent, but I said to myself that I am going to break the cycle that I grew up in and wanted something better for my children. My children wanted to know why I just very seldom would allow them to spend the night over people's homes or why I took them out to a party when it had just started and picked them up before it ended. Not because I was strict, it was because I was afraid due to the scary things I went through as a child. Don't get me wrong, I had some great times as a child too. Those scary times frightened me so that I didn't think about it. Because of my childhood, I would be afraid before I had children, that I would not know how to become a good parent. There is one thing I did learn. I could never please my children, and I soon learned quick in my thoughts when a child asked me for something or want me to do something. If you draw the line for that very moment, the child will not like your decision because they always want to do what they want, but they know they must ask their parents/parent or someone who is taking care of them, and they are always hoping you will go with their flow. I know because who would want to be told no (smile). I am on the roll with writing this week. Sometimes I may not write anything for weeks. Someone once told me what comes to mind use a tape recorder and record it if you are not in the writing mood. My response was I do have a tape recorder in my purse all the time. I do not use it to record things. I brought it because one choir director passed away only after working with him for a year and said we should invest in one. I never thought that it just may come in handy for book writing. I may use it because I need to catch my thoughts at the very moment. Today, I went to visit a church in the neighborhood, and the pastor spoke on the seasons of life.

Today, the church pastor I visited spoke on the topic "I don't have anything to wear," and then she told the phrase and brought it in a biblical point of view. Let's use that term again for encouragement to go out and live our life. Today, I got up and had an errand to run before going to church. It was a beautiful day; spring was in the air. Yet I had on some burgundy corduroy pants and a black pullover top with a picture of a pumpkin with pics of candy corn (which was one of my favorite candies by the way too bad you can only find them in certain times of the year). I sure did not feel like dressing up going to church today. I almost went to church dressed just like that. When I went home and put on a pretty dress, there were more people who are dressed down there than up. One time, I was invited to a very important event and was sent in an e-mail at 4:00 p.m. to attend an event the next day. I wanted to go to this professional event. I had no job but was getting unemployment. My hair was not done, and I was not the type who can do magic with my hair. I thought to myself I did not have anything to wear, and my hair was not done. I almost did not go.

I decided not to give in. I called my hairstylist at the time as she could do my hair. I looked in my closet and pulled out the prettiest black dress and my beautiful winter white wool coat and my Coach boots with lace in the back. Guess what? I was the hit on the event.

I did not know a soul. It was my first time meeting a person that the event was for. I got put together really quickly. My point was to check your wardrobe before you decide not to go anywhere, and you may find something dazzling or even when you're casual, there may be plenty of people who are in their casual wear. Season in life was brought up in a church I visited today. I truly believe that I am traveling at the beginning stage of new season for me. I do understand now that some people may not be traveling with me. They were only there with me for that particular stage. I wore my heart on my sleeve, but what can I say? As I continued to work writing on my book, there are some public issues that are shocking to a lot of people including myself. On April 20, 2016, I was reading that the prohibition of Harriet Tubman, who helped slaves escaped, is going to be on a $20 bill. This was very unusual because the only people on the monies are presidents. This was so historic that a former slave who traveled back and forth to free the other slaves did not have a holiday but is on money. Hopefully, this can be a start of the country in getting better by the way some people have been treated in the past and the present. Today on April 21, 2016, the great entertainer/singer Prince passed away. He was only fifty-seven years old. May he rest in peace. Life is too short.

We have to forgive and forget when and where we can. Sometimes, we get hurt in life. It does not mean that we should continue to hang out with people who do not add to our happiness. I wondered if in certain situations when I am struggling is that a sign from God that he has another plan better than the situation I am in. Sometimes, when I am tired of running in my place in life, maybe it is time to be on another agenda. It's certainly funny that when I'm struggling on the road of life. There was always this feeling in my spirits that I should be doing a whole lot better than what I was doing. I was not even thinking about writing a book, but I did ask others to about perhaps they should consider writing a book about themselves. I think most of my thoughts would always be to try to do the best I can. Sometimes, I would feel alone, but sometimes, I have to keep moving. What I have learned in life is that everyone you would be friends with may not want to be friends with you. Don't force, leave it alone. Sometimes, when one is trying to be friendly and help people, and it is not appreciated, one tends to feel disappointed. I know I do. When I was younger, I would think that people can learn to like you. Acceptance was always a big deal to me. I know that everyone is not going to like everyone; it's something that must be accepted and learn to move on. Today is Saturday. I remember being without full-time work for two years. I thank God that I am still living in the same home that I had fought so hard to stay here. On this note, let me talk about my home. This was a lease-to-own type of setup matter of fact that's what it was. After two years, I do have the option to buy, but I did not have a clue where to go to get help. The organization that ran the program did not have classes on how to prepare to own a home. I was a struggling single parent, so my finances were not the best. I tried every possible resource and get your finances together program I could get into, but still I rented the home. I prayed about it. I even put holy oil on the home sometimes, I would fall behind on rent, so the next time I got paid, I knew that the bulk of my check would have to go to the rent. The most memorable time was when the children were small, and one January, my gas got cut off, so at night, in order for my three children to stay warm even though they each were blessed to have their own room, but we had to sleep in my room in the same bed and load up our blankets and coats. The two youngest ones in the middle. Where was their daddy at? Unfortunately, he was in jail, and most of his jail stuff to my understanding was regarding traffic. He helped us when he could even have helped with the rent before or even found a money order to pay the rent that I had misplaced at home. We never got married, but the decision for us to part ways was the most liberated thing that I had ever done in my life besides writing this book. It's funny when my family tried to look for my downfall; they would make jokes about my children's father. To me, it is never too late to follow your dreams. I never understood why the more the struggles, the harder the struggles become. I was so concerned about my blood pressure. I went to the doctor and found out that I was okay. I have not been doing exercise at the gym like I used to. Never let the weight of your trouble drain you and take away your me time. Right now, it's a Saturday, and I am so relaxed and feeling great. Never be intimidated by your dreams; they are your dreams and go for them no matter how long it takes. I learned some things in my life. Sometimes I would say I have always fought for everything I have gotten, and there were times when I grew tired, but God never allowed me to give up. I do not know why it is taking so long for me to start dating again. I do not want to be dating just to be dating, but the dating to have must have true meaning and the man must be sincere. I say for the single people, never be desperate even to go out with a married man. I have not dated a married man before. Always look good even when you are not feeling the goodness. When you keep trying, I noticed the goodness comes around. Exercise is so important even if you do a little of it at home. I remember with my first child, I had to put my job on hold so I could be home with her. (She has grown up to be quite an independent young lady. She also graduated from college in 2014.) The maintenance man said to me that I was the only person that stayed at home and did not gain weight. I told him that is because I do exercise. To me, exercising makes you feel so much refreshed. I have my youngest daughter graduating from a university, and my youngest child is inspired to be an inventor and rapper. I live in the city in the same house for over twenty years. I fought to be able to stay in the same house. I came so close to moving years before I became the homeowner. I almost signed a lease somewhere. The landlord actually came to the house, but I did not sign the papers. The reason why we were moving was because my children had three cats, and they were attached to them, and I did not know they could not have them. Now since I am a homeowner, it feels great. This week has been tough, but when things get tough, you got to be tougher. Sometimes, when you think it gets easy when your little ones get older, sometimes, it gets harder.

I remember a saying that someone used to say when a child of theirs had grown up. Sometimes, things happen socially, and it would affect the parents. I went to work a couple of months ago, and I was told I left the window open by mistake, and a former friend of one of my children came through the window and had done damage to my home, for example, the cords were cut in half. Walls and doors were damaged, and I was a single struggling mother.

Sometimes, people do not care about other people, and yes, even your own family can try to destroy you by destroying what you work so hard to maintain. One thing that I did not like was to have to constantly replace the same thing over and over again. To me, that money can be used to purchase something different than to have to replace items and repair things that have been damaged. Sometimes, things may get me down, but I just keep on trucking. Keeping on trucking was a popular soul song back in the 1970's. The word itself was so strong and meaningful that there was a cartoon with a very large foot going forward. I believe there can be a message in that cartoon. Keep on trucking to me means when I see that large foot coming forward, meaning that progress is there waiting for the rest of you to come forward. You know you want to get there. All the struggles you've been through must take a giant step forward to keep on trucking because that's the only way you are going to make it. The cartoon had no one with, just the large foot stepping before the rest of the body came forward.

I also interpreted this cartoon as sometimes, when you make a move, you may have to make it alone, but it's you who take that giant step, you're going to make it, so give it your all.

I wrote something the other day. No matter how old you get, you just cannot accept some things. This is what I wrote: just my thoughts. It's funny when you know when someone does not like you for whatever reason. I remember coming to my mom as a little girl bringing this same thought. Momma said, "Everyone is not going to like you." Unnecessary meanness never till this day sit too well with me. To me, it was much easier to be kind than to be mean. I read somewhere if memory serves me correctly that more muscles are used to frown than it is to smile. Take for example when you are at work, people should try to work together because some people's work hours are put in for so long they see their coworkers more than their families. We might as well use the term work family.

A couple of months ago, I had a dream about birds. They flew to my window. I googled dreaming about birds and looked on YouTube. I'm not saying that these two are the gospel, but they did say similar things. Basically depending on what type of birds and what the birds are doing in the dream. It basically means that a person is going through a different stage or phase in life. Letting go of something for the better. One word that was used was transcending or escaping something. Going to another phase of higher spirituality. I am glad I am feeling better this week than the last. I got a temporary job working with washing and cleaning cars. I was throwing up. I wanted not to stop working.

Since the last time I wrote something in my book, so many lessons and words of encouragement can help inspire someone. I do not know where to begin. I attended my youngest daughter's graduation. The university has a very tough curriculum; it's in the state of New York. I know I could not have graduated from there. However, who knows if you put forth the effort, you just might make it. I notice if I work to pay the bills, I can also work hard to complete this book and always think of ways to improve my life. I learned a lesson in the past two weeks. Just because you think you know everything there is to know about yourself, it's like waiting but there's more. I found out recently that there is false information on my driving record. It was like unbelievable, when looking over my paperwork, making some changes with my insurance agent, the paperwork has false information about me. It said 12/2/2013. I was at fault accident, and it said three points, but I never hit anyone up to this date. Now I got paperwork, and I must straighten this out. I should have zero points. It's a lesson to me to do spot-checks on my driving record. The bad part about it was, I just recently found out. I have to check with the Department of Motor Vehicles (DMV). It's a good idea that once in a while, like one might run their credit report, check your driving record as well. Working for other people can be really tough. Sometimes taking the same mental beat down after mental beat, one might say maybe this current situation is only temporary and not to be permanent. I learned my lesson not to start hanging up awards and certificates. Do not get too comfortable. I even worked at one job, and they did not want anyone to see pictures of their families on their desk.

If you are not where you want to be in your career, keep trying because eventually, you will find where you'll be satisfied. If you have a job and not satisfied with it, work the job like it was the greatest job you ever had while looking for something else. So much has happened since the last time I begin writing this book. No, I am not dating again. Summer will be officially here. I had been under so much stress and strain that for a few weeks, I had no desire to work on my book nor to even think I could complete, but how could I lose faith in myself like that? Some days' stress and mental beat downs will do that to people. I had to be strong if I want to do the things I do. The rest of the day is not promised. Every second of the day should be counted, and days that are my off days I do my best to make it my stay-on-my-game days. I learned in life that no matter how hard I try and no matter how I thought I made a difference, there is always going to be someone in the wings that's not going to give you credit. Some of those very people that patted you on the back will turn that pat on the back into a stab in the back. I hope this book will sell well because not only the people that like you will buy the book, there will be people who do not like you who will eventually contribute in purchasing a book about you someday, just so they can learn more about you.

I had one person telling me years ago that I just float in someplace. I never thought of myself like that. Hopefully, they will buy my book and say, "Wow, she really did have to struggle," and I would have never guess it. Okay, this is what inspired me to do my book at this very instant. It was Father's Day, June 19, 2016. The basketball team Cavaliers was in game 7, the final game against the Golden State Warriors, which the Cavaliers won the championship. The Golden State Warriors won three games, and the Cavs won one. Statistics showed it was impossible for the Cavs to come back; it has never been done before. The Cavs just kept playing to win the championship. Game 5 the winner was Golden State, three games; Cavs, two games. Then game 6, if they had not won, there would not have been a game 7, and the Golden State Warriors would have been the NBA champion. Cavs had won three games like the Golden State Warriors had. Then game 7 came, and they won. The Cavaliers, to my understanding, has not won an NBA championship since 1964. They kept trying. Their story was so much that it inspired me to start back on working on my book and get a handle on the others' accomplishments. Artists need and thrive on encouragement because sometimes, it seemed like one is running on a treadmill. Another sad loss when the world has lost the famous world heavyweight champion of the world Muhammad Ali. He was seventy-four years of age. He was right around the and close in age of my very own parents. I have a mother, father and a stepmother. My mom had been in and out of the hospitals and nursing home. At first, it was a very hard pill to accept and swallow that this strong tough woman, after she retired, just slowly her health was not as good. Since the last time I made an entry in the book, my father and stepmother were on a plane trip to one of the casinos in Oakland. Now I hope the next thing I am about to talk about will be a lesson to someone. I know it was a lesson to me.

When I went to visit my father and stepmother at the casinos, I gambled even though I am not a gambler. I got so caught up in the winnings and the crowd circling around me I wound up leaving with no money in my pocket. I started spending $20 then I won $42. I gambled again, and my ticket had me down to twenty-four cents. I gambled again and had $78, gambled again and the total on my ticket was $324, then I gambled again and lost it. Then I got $224 then I lost it and walked out of the casino at 1:00 a.m. with no money, and my parents were already headed back to New York. My dad and step- mother had boarded their plane and left the casino at 7:00 p.m.

Something else had happened too. You think you are over how you were abused by the hands of a family member. Sometimes, it darkened your doorstep. We had a couple of family emergencies, and for my abusers to being there staring at me, I just could not look at them. They say never give your abusers power over you. The last time I saw one of them during a family tragedy, I thought to myself isn't he sorry for the way he treated me? I really do not know his age. He showed up at everything I had like the rest of the family. Wasn't he ashamed? Did he think it was okay to sexually abuse and beat on his little cousin? Why did he do this? He used to tell me that bad things will happen to him because I was a witch. The abuse started when we visited Oakland, and it has only gotten worse when my mom moved us to Oakland, and we lived with our cousins for two years.

CHAPTER

4

I REMEMBER WHEN MY FAMILY SAW me off to get back
on the bus headed back to the university, the very one that was so
mean to me growing up walked away crying. Did the past haunt
him? Maybe one day I will have the strength to ask him why, or did
I try to bury it. It is hard for me to explain to my children why I
never brought them around that part of the family. I never wanted
what I've been through to happen to them. My children, when they
got older, would get upset with me, because they did not understand
why I did not bring them around certain part of the family.

I hope that my book does not offend anyone because its purpose is to help someone else and to show I have grown up through
the struggles in my life. I know I could not have done it without God
because for some reason, when I was a child and became very ill, I
always got down on my knees and pray, and that was the first time I
have ever seen my mother cry, and I have not seen her cry since than.

So much has happened that has inspired me to start back working on my book since the last time I made an entry. The harder I try
my professional life and people do tell me I haven't done nothing. For
anyone that has their own business, I think that is such a smart busi-

ness move. I met a professional person with his own business, and he said to me that he didn't have a college degree, but he believed that a college graduate should be getting their own business. I know myself I had to start from scratch so many times with new jobs. Sometimes, you have to think like the old slogan Timex watch "It takes a licking and keeps on ticking." Every time I think this is a profession where I can get comfortable, it's like I cannot. Maybe God is trying to tell me not to stay there. I am there to assist in what needs to be done and move to the next chapter in my life. I am inspired to continue my story and will not treat it as another one of my false hopes. "I need to dream bigger than the dream."

I was just thinking every job that I have worked with, I have always got to the bottom of issues. I have worked a job that was in such bad shape it was like trying to bring it back to life. It was very tough, but it was done. Teamwork is very important, but the most important thing is to stay strong when the negative winds blow in. Sometimes, when I would think to myself this is the type of place I would want to retire at, then things happened that got me to thinking maybe God does not want me to stay here. I was always taught that when you work for an employer, you work like you are doing service for God. I believe in God. I have come so far in life, but yet I know I have so far to go.

Sometimes, I think that I should have so much more in life than I have, but I appreciate what I have. Some say I am too hard on myself, but I have learned not to worry as much.

I learned never stay anywhere just because you refuse to be running out of anywhere. You have to do what makes you happy. As I hear people in their senior years or golden years going back to college and graduating or getting a GED, that is wonderful. Like the saying goes, nothing beats a failure but a try. I was a prime example of giving out advice but not using that advice for myself. I decided to take my advice. I was satisfied with doing a couple of things in life, but in the back ground of my soul, I felt that I should be doing something more beneficial, but I could not put my finger on it. Maybe this too is just the beginning of a new beginning. Something in life I have finally learned is not getting all worked up over something you cannot change. As I listened to people debate about books, one was on the radio asking whether or not the author had written about things that should not have been told.

Zest for life should be something that does not go away with time. No matter how many times life knocks you down, just keeping trying. You sometimes may have people around you that think you should be feeling just as bad as the situation. Life is too short every day that I open my eyes I truly want to be a better person than I was the day before. When I am blessed to open my eyes, I am so grateful that God has given me another day to do better and to be better. I created a new group on LinkedIn called Authors Place. It is a place where writers can go and start a conversation. The first name I chose was Writers Den than Writers' corners I like Authors Place better. I always thought that I'll just be doing something that will benefit people. People can learn from it. I was a Sunday school teacher for about thirty years, and no matter what was going on in church or at home, I enjoyed teaching the children as much as they enjoyed hearing about God. I also sung in the choirs. I noticed the more you sing, the better your voice becomes. It is so funny, it so true that history repeats itself.

Clothes tend to look better if you have not worn them in a while and use the phrase "this old thing." There was one point where I had no church home I was no longer attending the church where I was baptized at. I was just visiting churches. At this point in my life, I see myself visiting churches more on a regular basis in my own neighborhood. There was a movie that coined these phrase, "Sometimes, life can be hard for no reason at all." I believe in God, and I would pray for better days. I see that better days are here each time I open my eyes. I hope that one day in the mist of creating my book, that God has groomed the person for me, and he has groomed me for that person, but if not, then God knows best (like the saying goes Father knows best).

As I struggled to complete a book that I truly want to complete, I think about one of my children. One of my children who just recently graduated from Colgate University. She had to do a twenty-eight-page paper in Spanish; she also had to turn around and do another paper with a lot of pages. On one of the social media sites, someone spoke on their concerns about performance evaluations. They spoke on how they worked, and her supervisor gave her unattainable goals and rated her very low. People in our social group spoke about how they thought the evaluation was unfair. I do not like evaluations because sometimes, it may not define the truth and depict the work of a person.

So much was happening in the world. I currently live in Oakland, California as I mentioned before. This is the time of the year when history is all over the place. This is the first time in decades that one of basketball teams has won a championship.

The group I started on Linked-in social media is called Authors Place. This group is for beginning authors and for authors who want to give advice. I started this group because I myself can get distracted by the hardness of life, and success sometimes is too far away. It only looks far away if you allow it to be far away. Sometimes, it is easy to be afraid of success especially when you have hardly any in your corner. You have to be strong. Sometimes to me, the harder one may struggle to be successful in what they do, it gets harder. Maybe it can be hard because more encouragement is needed these days. Sometimes, one can encourage others and do something for others, and even though one may not want anything in return, but showing that someone cares can go a long way. All I ever wanted in life is to be happy. I know that happiness is not always going to be a bed of roses. Sometimes, one has to let people go if he or she has tried so many years to be kind to them, and they do not want to accept one, they can very well become part of the reason of your unhappiness. I still am so excited about this book, and I am hoping that this book will help someone who has been through something. Sometimes, people may say this should not be said, you can lose this or that people will look at you differently. My philosophy is, and I am not a philosopher, if a person of a certain group of people who don't like you or want to create trouble if they find imperfect in your life, no matter how, they will make a big deal out of every mistake that you make even though they make mistakes, they try to destroy someone's character. The thing is continuing, so just do your best; and if they have the authority to make people think you aren't up to scale, believe in yourself and others will too. Goals should always be in the plan. Every day I have plan, a goal. This week, I picked days out of the week I will work on my book. I want to go ahead and finish it. I have asked people if they have goals, and sometimes, they do not have any goals. Why? I do not know. I would tell them to start out small. That I do started small working toward my goals. I asked myself where I see myself one year from now, or where do I see myself five years from now. Every month, I picked a couple projects I need to or want to achieve. Even if I fall back from something, I think on how I can handle the situation. Self-confidence is so much needed in the world because there are so many hidden talents that one may have, but their spirits have been beat down for so long that it takes a toll. A perfect example in the movie *The Wiz* where the crows were not afraid the of the scarecrow. In fact, they had the scarecrow so convinced that he could not better himself, and he was just found hanging on the pole not doing anything. Then Dorothy came along and showed the scarecrow a positive way in life. If you ever feel alone in a room full of people, you are actually not. A long time ago, I told someone I was sitting by myself, and I was alone. The response was that I was not alone, and that there was a room full of people.

Sometimes, you have to be a friend to get a friend. Education is so important. Everyone may not want to go to college. Getting a high school diploma or GED, with either of these, you can choose how you want to take your career or education from there. Courses in college can accelerate one's future and career. It's always good to dream, but dreams can come true. Some dreams may happen sooner than the other. Sometimes, obstacles can get in the way; sometimes, finances may play a part. Continue to persevere, and something positive is bound to happen.

Paying bills is so important. Sometimes I get swamped with bills. It's good to keep up with all your receipts. I thought maybe it's better to go old school and pay $5 that shows you intend to pay. Never ignore a bill collector's phone call. When you are young, people will offer you all kinds of credit. If one decides to get a credit card, try not to run them up. Some of my credit cards got ran up helping people, and yes, I brought myself clothes too, working part-time making $3.35 an hour while going to college. I was so young, and my bills were so high. Someone told me about an agency that can help me consolidate. It's funny, and then again, it is not funny when people see that you are doing well when in fact you are not. I remember having no lights and gas, and people would drop me off at home not even having a clue that my utilities were off.

No matter what the struggles we have, we must be determined to persevere. Sometimes, I would work on two jobs. The first part-time job was when my children were very small. I would pick them up from day care, get them dinner and then take them to the child-care. My shift was part-time after work after a full-time job. My first car I put $1,300 down on it, but it drove me into my first part-time job. There was so much wrong with the car, I had to get a second job. Even if chances look slim to get a better car, try looking a little further, maybe a few weeks longer. Maybe if I did, it would be alright and got a better car. I was always taught that if you really want something, save for it. I decided that I do my best to help others when I can, I need to help myself as well. I have learned to try not to panic. I am watching this old movie in it asking for the children to laugh, man or husband to dance and then the woman asked the wives to do something I did not hear because by ten pm, I was wondering what happened to me in my life, why how I am not married. I cannot remember the time I had been on a date. Sometimes, I know I should not worry about finding my "soul mate." Maybe I will, maybe I won't. I know there are people in the world who are middle-aged and find love again. I have had so many downfalls in life, but by the grace of God, these falls in life motivate me to turn them around to positive. Children are a blessing. I know a sad story where a woman had several children; unfortunately, she did not stay married. I have nothing against the woman; I am not judging her, but her family seemed to adore her, embrace her, but the woman did not treat her children properly. Even though she did not treat them right, she expected them to do whatever she wanted and do all kinds of wonderful things for her. If they did not, she would not want to deal with them. She was not supportive of them going to college or finishing high school. Most of her children did not finish high school, had children at an early teen age. These children loved their mother so much because after all, that's all they had. This woman was so mean when she could no longer care for herself, she was still being mean but extremely mean to one of her children. When her children were young, she would drop them off with anyone just for the sake of being with a man or going out and having a good time. To my knowledge, those children loved their mother. A lot of responsibility was placed on the oldest child; as the child begin to become an adult, they still cannot feel the parent's love that the oldest and the siblings truly deserve. It is no one's fault the father tries to be a better person than he was years ago.

She would often be leaving them with the family when one day, realizing that as she betrayed her own children, her family betrayed her by talking about her rudely and abusing her little ones. The question I have if parents don't have the respect for or the love for their own children, what makes them think that a family may have possible issues of their own, even respect for the children. I am no doctor, maybe the woman has had a tough child hood herself and perhaps never learned how to love herself. I am not a perfect parent, but I raised them children to do well. I am putting this in my book because I am so amazed how some people can be so cold. Some people want everything, but do not know how to give. There are some people who try to treat people the way they want to be treated. When I treat people the way I want to be treated, I am hoping I made a difference in someone else's life, and in the process hoping that I can be a better person. This woman today has gotten so ill, and through her illness, she still managed to be so mean to some of her adult children. Some people never change. Being a single parent can be tough, but prayer helps a lot. I believe in the power of prayer.

I did not know which way I wanted to go with this book. I just hope that things get so much better in life and in the world. Again, it's such an eye-opening era to be living in. I found out that I am not the only parent who slept on the couch waiting for their child to come home. Life is so tough these days for years. There was a bus stop in front of our home and across the street. Now they are going to discontinue the bus stop. Times are so dangerous I hope the transit system would have reconsidered. It was very convenient for people to catch the bus. Sometimes, you can talk till you are blue in the face, and some people do not listen to you. So much is happening out here even within your own house-hold. I don't sleep well until I know all my young adult children are in their designated places and are safe. I know I need to get off the couch and go to sleep, but when one of my children are still out in this dangerous world, it's hard. Enjoying life is good. It is good to go somewhere and have fun at least once a week if not at least once a month. When you are working and you are on a budget, try not to overload with a lot of clothes. If you are on a budget, buy a couple of outfits especially if you need them for work; there are a lot of great deals out there. Ordering from a catalog is not so bad since a lot of clothes do fit. I have ordered something from catalog, and a lot of time it works. Sometimes, if something does not fit, return it quickly. I made a mistake of just holding on to something in hopes that it would fit; I just return some things if I see nothing there that I like or if I get another size. If you hold on the items, you may not be able to fit into it. Maybe the design is made to fit a certain type of silhouette.

Sometimes it's very difficult looking for a job and landing the one you think you should. Some people think it's because of our skin, sometimes it's because of too much skills or lack of skills, sometimes in the wrong city or at the wrong company. One has to keep on trying. These days, it's not over; once the children are grown-up, it's starting all over again. You make sure you do something every day. Even if you are cleaning your house or working on a new idea. Life is for the living, so live it if you are not already doing so. Some things I learned in life came from some advice people give you. Some are good for that time and current situation; some are not to be continued for a life time. When you work always, give it your all. After all, someone is paying one to do a certain job. It used to be got the job done and go home. Most wanted your job because you make it look easy even if it was very difficult. Sometimes, some people just met to get your own business. It's so much out now; you can do it now, success beyond running a store or inventing something in order to be successful. Although running a store or creating an invention is great. It's so funny I went on a one-day shopping trip recently, and I got to visit and eat lunch at a mansion that is a copy of the famous movie *Gone with the Wind* mansion. There were exhibits from the movies and the pictures. There was one picture that stood out in my mind, and that was the picture of Scarlett O'Hara after they lost everything. There was a scene when she was very dirty, and she said, "I will never go hungry again." Some knew what it's like to have no choice but to be hungry with no money and no food. I have been hungry so many times, but the time that I was hungry the most was before I had children; and when you were single, back then you were allowed to get little help. I was going to college, and I was staying in a house with no lights and no gas. It used to be a home where all my siblings lived in including my mother, but she split the scene and did not tell us the problems we were in. One of my brothers, which I will not mention his name, unfortunately, with everything we had to endure together, growing up sad to say we were not close, but I love my siblings, and I have always helped them at some point in time in my life. I mean that is what family does. I was more concerned about my family more than I was myself. I remembered one time my mother asked me to take my two sisters. I could not believe she asked me that. I was struggling going to college and already had my brother living with me, and I only had two bedrooms. My thought was why would she give her children away to another child that was struggling herself at that time I was in my twenties.

Social media is a good place to keep up with family, friends, and to promote things. While I am writing my book, I let my family and friends on social media know I hope they will purchase it. I know everyone that you know on your social media page is not your friend. Sometimes, they use it against you. I had a couple of people when I see them, they would make negative remarks about my social media page. I just remove that person off my page because I wanted no trouble. I just removed them. Sometimes, when you are trying, you may get people who say negative things about you that you just say to yourself what have they done so spectacular in their lives that they would try to discourage you. Just remove them from your page if you feel guilty. Just think back at what type of relationship you had with the good and bad. These days, I do not like to say, but you must love yourself because there are going to be so many times that self-love is all you are going to have. Planning at a young age was what I loved to do. To my surprise, it certainly did not turn out like I had wanted to. My dreams and plans would have put me right where I would had comfortably ever after. Sometimes, things happen for a reason. I probably would not have written this book. My life would have been one big secret; my abusers would have thought that what they did to me was okay, and if they abuse me, there are others there who were abused and mistreated as well. It is never right to hurt anyone in any type of shape, form or fashion. If someone is in your care, that is just what it means, you care for them. If people from out of town know what's going on. How did they know but yet the caretaker continues to leave the ones that they care for in the wrong hands, just for a moment of freedom from them, but yet they are someone in the abusive hands. In my opinion, it's never too late to dream.

I see so many articles about people in the eighties who are getting their high school diploma. When I attended a university, there was a sixty-five-year-old woman who lived on campus working on her bachelor's degree. I am writing this book to inspire others, and it's inspiring me to carry on. One of my favorite quotes are "Surround yourself with people that is going to lift you higher," and "You can make it if you try." One of my late uncles passed away so young at fifty-two years old. He was the only uncle I got to grow up with. One of his quotes was, "Hang around with people who are doing better than you so you will do better yourself." When you do not feel like doing something, just get out and do something possible. I try to be kind to everyone who I come in contact with.

I never knew someone's story and what kind of life this person has encountered. Sometimes, people tend to judge a book by its cover. Like I've been struggling, people tend to judge me thinking I am doing so well. Maybe I am too hard on myself, some people say I am too hard on myself. I stay late for work all the time. I am working on leaving when I should be leaving. Never married, and my three children have the same father. I just listened to him recently saying he was never broke. His people would tell me he would have money, but yet a lot of times, the kids and me would be starving. I kept my children in church, and we prayed when we were in the car driving as well. I say me and my three children were going to go straight to the top. I remember I had to borrow $15 to buy food because there was no food in the house when I had my first child at that time. Maybe my baby was two years old. A college friend of mine took us to the store and brought us some food, and I saw her wipe one of her eyes as my child grab a piece of fruit out of the grocery cart and ate it before my friend could pay for it. My life has not always been good nor has it always been bad. I was always the one that thought getting an education was the way to a better life; even with my education, I was still suffering and struggling, and the man in my life made it no better. One day, I woke up and said no more getting back together and breaking up and getting back together, breaking, and it's over, it's wrap up. I thought to myself just maybe my life will get better and will do better. Even with no man in the household, I arose to the occasion. I know I did not want my children living the type of childhood that I had. I did my best not to bring them around people that if they did not treat me right, they may not treat my children right. I was determined to break the negative terrible cycle of bringing my family in to what anything goes in the atmosphere and doing so without care. When my children were young I hesitated about allowing them to spend the night over anyone's home because of the abuse and trauma that I experienced as a child. I think that one of my children's God mother may have even picked up on it because one day, she said, "Let your child spend time with us." I do not remember the exact words, but basically, she said, "We will take care of her," so at that point, how do I allow my child to spend more time with them? I did trust them always. I just wanted my children and I to spend time together. Time that I have never gotten from my parents. My dad is still alive, and he was trying to make amends. My mom's health is not too good, and every time I see her she's so mean to me, and that's something that has always been that way ever since I was a child. This book is about me, and my thoughts are for people who need to know how I grew up as a child. This is not a personal attack on my parents, this is a self-help book, about how I rose out of the ashes and lived my life and learned to love myself. What are the odds of me not becoming a heavy drinker or even a drug addict? God watched over me. Till this day, I have struggles and battles. I asked God to advise me and help me through. I became stronger, but I do believe if my dad and I lived in the same city, my life would be different, maybe even better. Like I told my mother, this book is about me, and this is a self-help book. The Lord saved my life so many times. I remember when I was in the sixth grade, I was really sick in school. I had a fever too. I remember my mom and her boyfriend picked me up from school. At that time we were staying with my family, she dropped off me and continued on her way with her boyfriend. I stayed in her room for three days; she did not come back to the house to check on me. Day three, my great aunt told me, that I have to get up and get something to eat. I had not eaten nor drinking anything for three days. God bless my great aunt, she was my grandfather's sister. I never had met my grandfather. Grand dad died from working in a factory, due to the fumes that closed his throat he was in his mid-twenties. My grandmother died, from a home abortion, when my mother and her brother were small children. Every Sunday, we had to say the Lord's Prayer and read scripture from the Bible. She passed away. My great aunt rest in peace. Great aunt rest in peace. I was told by another relative that my great aunt said that I really was going to make something out of my life. I love everyone even though I know everyone I come in contact with is not going to love me or even like me. Like what my mom told me when I was a little girl coming home from school upset that some of the girls in school did not like me for no reason. Her words were "not everyone is going to like you." I enjoyed feeling free and just being myself, not caring anymore who likes me or not. I learned it's okay to stay away from people that who truly do not mean you well. I was taught as a child by a neighbor on the street to never run away from your troubles. If you start running now, you will always be running. At that time, I was twelve years old. My friend's mother gave me advice talking to me over the telephone. At the age of twelve, after that phone conversation, I always stood and faced my battles head-on. We were bouncing back and forth from New York to Oakland on a regular basis, and I felt it was time for me to get ready to bounce back to the other city, but my friend's mother conversation that one evening put a different outlook in my life. Sometimes, you have to learn to embrace yourself and learn to love yourself. Self-respect starts at home; you respect yourself, and your family and others will respect you and yours too. What I learned in life is if something is not working for me, it's okay to step out of that environment. I truly feel blessed with everything I have been through in life. When I was a teenager losing sight of myself I was hanging on to the Lord. I got down on my knees and started praying. I believe in God, and through my experiences and especially what I have been through as a child, there was nobody but God who brought me out and brought me through. About twice in my life I felt this void one time before I had children and the next time after I had children.

The first void prayer to God was asking him what should I do because there was this void in my life. I also asked in the prayer what he wanted me to do. I was visiting churches even though I was baptized at the age of twelve years of old; I was no longer going to the same church I used to go to. We moved out of the neighborhood during the summer I graduated from high school. The apartment building we lived in when I was twelve years old to seventeen years of age was being shut down. It already had the Condemn sign on. It was just a matter of everyone moving out soon as they find a place to live in. Getting back to the first void I started visiting churches, then I finally joined one after visiting it many times. The second void I had was not only a feeling that there was a space to be filled but something like a void and plus something else missing. I started writing a book less than a year ago. Right now, I know what needs to be done and what needs to be completed. I just need to complete it. At this point, I do not have a void. Some people think if you have not done something productive in life at a certain point, you have gotten too old. I totally think as long as I am able to get up and I should be like

I am blessed to see another day, I need to make it count. I remember that I have seen on social media that people celebrate people getting out of jail quicker than a person getting out of college. I do not condone wrongdoing, but back in the day, wrongdoings may have been holding hands with the opposite color. There were so many people in jail that found justice, but unfortunate for many years. The late great Nelson Mandela, the boxer, "the Hurricane" Rubin Carter, and so many others that were locked up in prison. I heard that there was a talk about solitaire in prison that was said to be cruel inhumane and should be done away with. There are so many young people in jail, or who are being gunned down for no reason especially young men. I fear for my only son. I do not even want him catching the bus because it's so dangerous. It's sad, in my opinion, that it's more dangerous out here with the young man than with the young woman. It's just not safe for no one these days.

It has been a very hot temperature this summer in Oakland, California. I am so grateful of the hot weather because winter in New York really cold. Things tend to be slowed down a little. Cars stuck in the snow. Being hungry or too full can have its disadvantages. I remember when I would be hungry for days in roll. A couple of times, I would have not eaten for three days in a roll in my early twenties. In particular time, I was going to college and had not eaten. Another time I was living in substandard housing that we were caught off guard, because, we, living with Mom, and she moved and left her things there, we did not know she was going to be moving out and had no idea as well as no utilities it was being about to condemn. We had received a letter that it was going to be shutdown. I had no children at the time, and I had gone to the public assistance building to see if I could get a housing voucher and some food stamps. The only job I had at the time at the age of twenty was making $3.35 per hour, one to ten a week and diligently working on my college degree. I ran into an old high school friend. I was not asking or begging her for money. I was just telling her my current situation and that I have not eaten anything in three whole days because I had no money for food. She handed me without a hesitation $40. I was so grateful. The most interesting time I was hungry for three days. I was in the welfare building, but I do not like using the word or term welfare building, be honest, it reminded me of a down-trodden-type situation. I believe if one can help it, get off the public assistance. Use it to better yourself not to make it a way of life. I remember once I got a car through the public assistance program, I got a $3,000 voucher to purchase a car. This was because I was a working single parent. The worker who was assisting me to get the car gave me the hardest time one could ever imagine. I was so frustrated by the difficult time the worker was giving me that I almost given up. She was talking to me very rudely to top it off. Since I have been conditioning to handle tough situation, I rolled with her. I did get a used car for about $3,100. So I had to pay the dealer the voucher for $3,000 plus out of my pocket $100, plus the tax on the car. My friend was so amazed I got the car. To my knowledge, the program to get a car is no longer in existence. They did not even advertise it much. I was watching the news, and they were talking about the program, so I gave it a shot. There are a lot of free things; we just have to look for them. If you are on a budget, try to buy a few pieces of clothing one or two through the month. It freshens up your wardrobe. When I worked in a major department store, it was great because I got some real nice designer pieces without the designer prices. Sales plus discounts on top of other discounts are a bonus. The red tag sales and additional off the tags like 65 percent off; the red tag was great. It was something how I went to college to work in a clothing store to become a manager or a buyer of clothes. I never got the opportunity to be in management; they always put me in sales, but the trickiest one of them all is to be careful when you are interviewing. I was applying for an assistant store manager position, and all throughout the interview, I truly believed that I was interviewing for the position. I asked if it was the assistant store manager position, and I was told no. My unemployment was about to run out with no more extensions, so I accepted the job. It was a part-time sales position, and it went by your sales quota. I was not bitter because of the situation. I just work the job I was looking for something else. I worked the position like it was truly what I applied for. I met some interesting people just by being a salesperson.

Sophie always wanted to take piano lessons as a child. While working in sales, I got a business card from someone who had a connection with music. Sophie started taking piano lessons and also got an athlete autograph. I just could not understand how a person can say and think "Sophie thinks she's something." They truly do not know anything about where Sophie had been and what she had been through and how long it had taken her to overcome many obstacles. She believed in God, and if it was not for the Lord, Sophie would not know where she would be. It seemed like she was not comfortable in the position because when something did happen, that had given her a wake-up call. Maybe God wanted her to stay there for a little while. Sophie, through everything and all the struggles, just knew how to stay prayed up. It's tough when your parents are ill. Sophie has always tried to do the right thing. Sometimes when growing up in a dysfunctional family, Sophie just wanted something different, something positive, the chance to be happy.

CHAPTER

5

SOMETIMES, IT SEEMS LIKE THE world is going backwards. Some people are still not treated right. Sometimes, it's like the old south all over again or the 1960s in the north. Independence and the Fourth of July really means something to the United States. Some people are not up to celebrate it. Maybe one time in their lives, they have celebrated it before, but due to so much killings and injustice, perhaps their minds have been hard and harsh of the world. I used to be very afraid of going to the dentist until recently. I mean I got my checkups, but a couple of my wisdom teeth stayed in until I had no choice but to get them removed. I had a swollen jaw and no car because it got repossessed. I had the car for five years, just borrowed money to pay for it, and filled it up with gas when the repo man took it and asked for the key. His son took off the plates within seconds. The car's worth was $21,000. Two months later, a new company sent a repo person out and said he was coming to pick up the same car. I found out that the old company was not supposed to be picking up cars. So I lost my first brand-new car sold at an auction for $3,000. I first got that car it was the same week/weekend of my birthday. I was not even planning on buying that car.

I look at it as a gift from God. The car that I trade in the gear stick fell out. I was at the church the security guard attached the gear stick back. I never heard of that in my life a gear stick falling out. I had just brought it used and did not even have it a month. I was without work for a couple of years, but I was blessed to get unemployment. I am not still making the money that I am accustomed to, but I know you are never too old to stop dreaming, stay on your course. Sometimes, things come up. I have also learned that everyone that hangs around you is not your friend. Some truly are and some are truly not. Sometimes, I have to get in my own world and just do my thing. I have a saying if you do not want anything told to them, do not tell it. Sometimes, things get out, and either it can help you or hurt you. Once when I was struggling, it seems like some of my hardest struggles was when I was growing up. I was working part- time and going to school. At that time, the minimum wage was $3.35 per hour, and that was what I was making. One day, I came home when I lived with my mother. One day, I got home, and there were no lights. I should have known this was going to happen, because at first, the gas was shut off. Eventually, she moved to live with her boyfriend. So I mentioned this to someone I was working with at the store how I was living. I was going to college every day and going to work on my schedule and living in a dangerous neighborhood with no lights and no gas. I told one person in this huge department store. The next thing I know, the whole staff in the department store knew. I asked my coworker why did she tell something that I told her in confidence, and her response was, "Sophie, it was something that needs to be told." At that point, I could not even be upset with this part, it's kind of choking me up. In times of need, know who your real people are. I even got a telephone call from another person in the department store letting me know that my little brother and I could stay with her. My brother was also in college as well; we attended two different schools. I did appreciate her offer, but I did decline. We had both been looking for our own separate apartment buildings. His place was ready two days before mine. I stayed with him for two days then my place was ready. I remember his landlord was so kind to us. Even though we were adults, I believe in his eyes we were two siblings trying to make it in the world and no support, but each other. I know God was with us the entire time. Bandits did not go into the house that the landlord had abandoned until we moved out of it. The house was like a four-family flat, it was full, but we wand up being the last two in it. We both finished college. Sometimes, I do not understand what happened to family that have been through so much. I have not heard from that particular brother in years; the other siblings we communicated in emergencies. Hardness of life either brings families closer together or tears them apart; this was our case, it's the latter. I never forget one Sunday in church, a soloist sung "Amazing Grace." It hit me so hard, I started thinking about this tough job I had to face the next day and how I missed my siblings. I just had uncontrollable sobbing. An usher came over, but I believe I looked like I really did not want her assistance (smile). Sometimes, life can be difficult as a child and not having the resources you need makes it difficult. I remember struggling in high school. My mother's boyfriend on the side was contributing to my high school graduation, but Mother also had live-in boyfriend as well. It was sad to say that they both tried to hit on me when I was a teenager. Mother was troubled that her side man was helping me, but it was not even my ideal, I was just a kid. One day, she said that was her boyfriend. Mother and I had more downs than ups. I watched over my sibling like they were my very own. I really did not have a choice. One of the neighbors who lived in the same apartment building that I lived in Oakland, California called my great-great auntie Rose and told her that she thought that Mother was treating me bad. I know this to be true because when I went back home to New York to visit Aunt Rose, she told me. I would always be so grateful to see her. She never had children of her own, maybe because God knew that she would have so many relatives to look after, watched over and take care of. I remember the summer after the university let out, I was going to stay the summer with her. Mother had told me that Aunt Rose had passed away. I went to her funeral, and it was a very sad time. She was truly the backbone of the family. Her husband passed away when I was a toddler. Mother used to tell this story about how fat of a baby I was, and every day when Great- Great Uncle Ted would come home from work and I would be so happy to see him, I would run and bounce on his leg that he would cross after a hard day at work. My dad remained in New York and has remarried. I wondered would life be different if Mother never relocated us to another city, and we got to see our father more? My father was trying to tell me one day out of the blue why he never paid child support. I heard the words starting to come out of his mouth that he wanted to pay child support, but I cut him off. I just did not want to know why after I was grown up and with my own family. You see, my father was such a liar, and next week meant never. It was so hard to believe the truth from the lie. My father came from the south, he came north where he and my mother met in New York. They married at such a young age. I heard of people getting married earlier than that. I have the upmost respect for my parents; they were not ready for children. My father did not know his temper. His anger and short temper could be his version of a spanky look like he is fighting in an old Western movie brawl in bar. One time, I made my father so angry because I said to him what my great-great auntie Rose said to me and I did not want the $7.99 shoes, I wanted the $14.99 shoes. He slowed the car down and slapped me in my whole face and then on my legs really hard. When I got out the car, I threw the shoes on the front lawn. He ran into the house with the shoes and started hitting me. He also hit me across the kitchen table then with my collar up, he torn my blouse so aggressively or should I say ripped it so bad that, why he still had me all collared up, I was trying to cover my bust. Uncle Leon was alive at the time. He is my mom's younger brother. Uncle Leon was home at the time. He heard the commotion in Aunt Rose's kitchen and race to intervene. Aunt Rose was sitting in the kitchen looking shock. I have felt pain like that since my abusive cousin punched as hard as he could in my chest when I was twelve years old for no reason. We all had to share the same bedrooms, the boys and girls. He used to sneak in the girls' bed very late at night. I was so frightened. This is the same cousin that molested me for many years, starting at the age of six up until I was fourteen years old. He was physically and mentally beating me and sexually abusing. He was one of the most vicious and violent cousin I had ever met. I do not know why he targeted me out, but he did. How can another child be so mean to his little girl cousin? I think he was about three to four years older than me, I cannot be sure. I could not tell my mother because she was rarely there, and I would have probably been beaten more. Abusive behavior is just never okay or normal to mistreat someone. Working is no longer over at the age of sixty-five years of age. People are working past the age of sixty-five years of age. I always enjoy working. I know this rich man in his nineties was well respected in the community, and he still ran his business and donated things to the community. When I went to see Momma at the rehabilitation center, she told me a few times that one day, I will be in a nursing home. My thought was, had she told all the siblings that? Everyone does not have the same health problems. I always wanted to do normal things with my mom, like always go shopping together even when I got grown. Our relationship even as a child was not the greatest. Maybe I disappointed Momma somewhere along the line. One time in my early twenties, she even said she was jealous of me. You see Momma never gave a second thought or even baby me after I got out of the hospital. The only thing she would say is that my sweet little girl had changed. Momma did not know because she was gone a lot that I never changed, but the hardness in my life as a child brought out the hardness from my inner self. Mother said to me that I can fit in anywhere. I just wish my parents really took the time to get to know who I was as a child and till this very day just be kind to each other. Even as I visited her in the nursing home center her room door was always close. She did not mingle with the rest of the people that participate in activities there. She was so mean to me when I went to visit her. Even when she had surgery years ago, I went to see her, she was so mean. Two out of the three children said they do not even like her because she was so mean to them as a child and as an adult. Then mother wondered why my children do not even go around her. As a child when I got so depressed I had to go into a psychiatric hospital. I saw her come and visit me, while I was in the hospital. She cried so bad; that was the first time, and only ever saw my mother cry. I never understood my parents. Some say it's my mother's fault I was in the hospital. You know what, I am okay now. I do not blame my parents for what happened to me and how we grew up. All was not bad. I got my mind back. I love helping other people. My father would tell me never to tell anyone that this happened to me about being in the hospital for a mental illness. People do treat you differently sometimes. I do not treat people differently. When I was in college, we were on the topic of abuse. Mental abuse was being talked about more and more. There are some people who need help and never got it. My cousin who abused me so bad when I was a child needed help. What sane person abuses and terrifies a cousin. He was a very handsome boy; he did not have to do those horrible things to me. He dated all the cool pretty girls. I don't understand why he did that. His personality was far from handsome. My mother just was not around to protect me from that. The other children in the house knew, but they took it very lightly, kids right? To me, it was a nightmare. Great-Great Aunt Rose, who was still living in New York at the time, may have tried to get me to talk about it. I was visiting her, and she said I am told that one of my cousins liked me. I never said a word. I wondered who told her, was it Mom? Others said because I was dropped off to too many different places that is what one of the people in the hospital said. If I looked deeper, as a grown-up woman, what did she mean? Was she trying to say about the way that some of the places we left or dropped off at we were possibly being abused or mistreated? We did not always know the fit of ourselves or others. I always tried to do my best to exercise more; sometimes, other factors cause poor health. I always tried to keep my medicine with me at all times. I developed asthma, and it had taken the hospital a year to figure it out I had asthma; allergy pills was good for me to have on hand. An illness can happen anytime and anywhere. When my children were little, I had not been in the clinic for myself in two years. I was saving all my time for my children in case I have to take them to the doctor or even have to stay home with my child who is sick. However, not many times my children were sick, but they did not get sick much. I sometimes work at a temp agency. This type of agency is strictly hard work. I never got stung by a bee in my life. I was washing cars on the weekend on an assignment from the temp agency, and I felt the most horrible pain I had ever experienced. I did not even see the bee on my arm. I never felt it on my arm, only the aftermath of it. It was a little after 10:00 a.m. and the shift had started at 8:00 a.m. I was scheduled to leave at 4:00 p.m. I was terrified about the sting. Bees and mosquitoes were very dangerous insects. You just do not know the outcome of it. I was told that there are a couple of types of bees, the honeybees, and the yellow jacks. I was told some people have severe reactions to a bee sting. I had not taken my allergy pill, so I took it. I washed the wound out with soap and water. The swelling went down, but I was humbly grateful that the sting was not deadly, or I had to go to the emergency room. I almost left the job to have it checked out, but I did not get any immediately allergic reaction, nor do I ever see the sting. It had been a couple several weeks since the bee sting, but instead of my skin being flat like it was when I thought I had the healing process figured out, it had now formed a small bump where the bruise was. I hope before I finish the book, the bee bruise will heal. I remember this movie and one of the spouses was really feeling down, and the other spouse said, "Sometimes, life can be hard for no reason at all."

Sometimes I may not cry about something or cry on the outside, but my soul inside sometimes cry. I should admit that there are times I get lonely. Some people I used to call every day I guess; sometimes people change or a life-changing event may happen and some of the people they once were closed to are no longer close. Sometimes, some people are only hanging around you for a short time and some for a long time. There are different journeys I have traveled through life, and sometimes, it can be clear because what they do for a living do not define who they are as a person.

I am not judging anyone because for me, people are people. I have met people who are very kind to me. I also believe that if you are kind, kindness will be returned. It is very difficult when you spent your entire life trying to better yourself, and it just seemed hopeless. You just have to keep trying. I believe in the saying "nothing beats a failure but a try," "if at first you don't succeed try, try again." I started working part-time jobs because I was out of work for a couple of years. I could not believe it. I was making great money for the position I had, and one day, I came to work and was told I no longer had that position. I asked the question what am I supposed to do, and the response my supervisor gave me was a shrug in the shoulder and the words "I do not know." I was getting unemployment for a couple of years, and then there was no extension of unemployment. I was blessed a couple of weeks prior to losing my unemployment. I had no choice but to take a part-time job. Sometimes in life, I realize that I have to and had to make lemonade out of lemons. It's nothing wrong with dreaming about what you want out of life and do not ever be sidetracked into thinking you are too old. I see people and hear about people going back to school past their being sixty years of age. Going back to school is not always about getting a college degree; it is also a dream for a person to get a high school diploma. Each day that one is blessed to open their eyes, make it count and always try to do better than you did yesterday. One day in a company meeting, I had been struggling to move up; in this particular company, it was a company-wide meeting, which was very crowded.

One of the executives were there, and she gave the employees an opportunity to speak, and I got up and spoke. As I spoke, I felt the executive was trying to shut me up, but I spoke from the soul about how strongly I felt about bettering myself. I would get up and exercise if it was a couple runs around the block or five minutes exercise before going to work. I stood up in the company meeting and said, "Every day I am blessed to open my eyes, I try to be a better person than I was yesterday." Sometimes I spend a lot of time wishing and hoping. I have prayed a lot. I do believe in the power of prayer. I remember one time in church, we had to walk up to the front, and we were giving donations. All I can hear was the silence of paper money falling to the donation basket. All I could muster up was fifteen cents, in which that was the only time I heard money fall into the collection plate. I wish that I could have given more, but that was all I had. I exactly know how I felt but being broke is never a good thing. Once you have a goal, it may be tough, but never give up on it. I know I have been taught to forgive and forget. It does not mean that I have to be around people who do not mean to me well. It means that I must continue my journey. So far, I never questioned why bad things happen. If one survives and can go on and live a productive life, it is truly a blessing. If you can open up and talk about it, and not care who judges you, well, they may be living in glass houses themselves. I was speaking to a group, and a topic came up about not getting along and the topic of arguing.

It took at least two people to argue. Sometimes, it's best to walk away or speak with a higher authority who can diffuse the situation. It so sorrowful out here in the world. When the saying goes "history repeats itself," there's so much sorrow in the world. Sorrow does not have a name on it. Sorrow hit my home again. As I am writing this book, I am going through something with my very own family. We can often have been told the dos and don'ts in life, but sorrow has no name. Sometimes when you may think you are doing bad, others see it differently. When my children were little, I wanted to have a decent car for them to be in. I was a struggling single parent, and I was blessed with my first new car, and it was fully loaded. The car was $21,000, which was a lot of money to me. I had lost my job and had not been out of work in years.

I had no clue what to do. Being a single parent and my three children were still very little in age. I went to the public assistance department, and the case worker started laughing at me. I did not understand at the time, but as days went by, I understood. He was a white man and myself being a hardworking single parent and a black woman, when he told me to go home and go to sleep, I was very offended. Perhaps he knew that I would no doubt probably that I would get unemployment. He told me to apply for unemployment, and I got it. I was just afraid of losing my job because I worked so hard in life. My life was nothing like I thought it would be. I had it all planned out in my head. I would think the term must be called a fantasy world I had created for myself. When I thought a man that was a go-getter and doing well for himself could be possibly interested in me, I would be happy, but only I find out this man was only either the term would be leading me on or just trying to be nice, or I accidently find out he has a girlfriend that isn't taking no stuff. I always thought I deserved a good man. I always hoped that all my kids went to college; two out of three is not bad. I always thought my son, my only son, my youngest, would be a famous basketball player.

They all are very smart despite being in a single-parent home. Their father had always been in their lives; he may not have been the best provider for them, whether it was money or selfishness, I will never know recently he told me that he always had a lot of money. Well, I remember there were days that my refrigerator did not have a lot of food in it, or we had to wait to 11:00 p.m. at night for him to bring or buy hamburgers if he showed. A person that was close to his family told me that my children's father always had money. This man had begged me to have children because when he met me, I had no children, and I was planning on moving back to New York once I got my bachelor's degree. He said he would marry me, but as I write this book, we have never gotten married. The closest we came to going downtown to city hall and getting an application to getting married. He loved his women too much I suppose. One day at this time, I was expecting my third child; we went on my lunch break to get the paperwork. I never forget something that upset him, and he ripped up the marriage license application right in my face, right in my kitchen. Somewhere along the line, I felt I could do bad by myself. When he asked me to go back to city hall, I told him no. I never regretted us not being married. Sometimes, we make poor choices in life. I always thought once I got tired of being dogged out by this man and disrespected, I would walk away. If I remove this man out of my life, the relationship was over, just maybe God will give me all my hopes and dreams back and just maybe my life would get better. Someone once told me I always see the good in everything. The good thing was in the relationship. I saw was my three children, and I love my children. I just want them to have a better life than what I had. I never really liked being fixed up with someone. It must be a catch while I am writing this book, someone is giving me the impression that they are trying to hook me up with one of their family members. I have not been on a date in years. At this stage in my life, I do not want to be dating for the sake of dating; I want a meaningful relationship, and I want a man who feel the same way.

I am putting this in my story because I have been seeing the person's family member to come visit his family. His family member asked me if I have seen him and told me all about him even when he's dating. Maybe she was just so proud of him. I haven't asked God to show me why this was happening, but tonight, I am going to pray to God to let me understand because it would be not good to think that they are trying to hook us up. Right now, I do not know if he's dating. He had a tragedy in his life. Sometimes, when we see each other, we speak. The last time I saw him, I was pulling up in my driveway, and I know I had gotten three shades darker (so my daughter told me) from working on a second part-time job in a temp agency. I had been washing cars all day. He looked at me, but he was on the phone. I did not look at him because last time, I smiled at him. The last time I saw him, he was with his family, and he smiled at me, but this time, it was not returned. You never know what a person was thinking. So we have to see. It seemed like I may not even be his type. From what I have seen in the past, he seemed to like brown-skinned women, and I am not brown skinned. Maybe it just seemed that way. Sometimes, people try to argue me about my race. Now after all these years, my mother said I have a lot of Indian in me. For years, she always told me I am black, so that's why I am black all the way. I have no color barriers, but to me, I think that everyone should know what they are. There are all these companies for money depending on how far you want to research your bloodline history. I remember a time when there were family trees that the elders kept, and it would tell you a lot about one's history. So much of that is gone now, speaking on a person's history the bloodline. It was getting a bit much and to me bold, when I was standing in line, people asked me what am I. I said black; they want to argue the point what my race is. Black people come in all sorts of colors. I get tired of people asking me my race, but I do not want to be rude, but I really want to say is that I am from the human race. I hope that I do get married one day, and we will always feel that we are the luckiest two people in the world. For the past several years up until now, I always thought that there was something great. I am supposed to be doing like making a difference in someone's lives or life. Maybe I have. I remember once years ago, a lady's son was trying to start a church. She asked me if they could use this chapel where I used to work, and I said yes. I got transferred, and I came back to old site the company that sent me away to another site for five years. It felt like I came back from a war. The same lady was still living there and told me how her son had gotten his own church and at that time had seven hundred members and had church vans. God is good once I so happened to ride behind one of the buses, so happy to be able to witness more soldiers on the battlefield for Christ. I tell you next time I am blessed to have a companion. I want us to go to a nice restaurant where we can talk and make each other laugh because I can truly use some happiness in my life. I hope he does too whoever he is. It is taking him a long time to show up in my life, but I prayed and asked God to send me a good man. I believe that he will, but I trust in God for so many things he has brought me through. I do not want to be alone for the rest of my life

I remember one of my cousins after not seeing her for a long time made light of my children's father and I for not making it. She didn't know the story. I just agreed with her and said that's right, and she sounded cheerful. This is the sister of my cousin who abused me and beat me up for many years. He had the nerve to want to befriend me on Facebook. I hope he did not think that what he had done was acceptable, but it was not. I have to see and accept what happens as far as me having a husband.

There are so many people caught up in the system of the law.

Sometimes, we hear through the media or maybe even know about someone who is innocent that had been in jail for years and finally been proven incorrect and even then some folks still do not want to let them out. Right now, my son is going through. We got him out on bond, and then they raised his bond, and I had to put our home up for collateral. We have a public defender, and he said that this will be like this until all of this is over. I asked how did we get here in this situation, hanging with the wrong people. I kept saying telling to cut that person off. He was hanging with the wrong people. If he had not gotten bailed out of jail, he would have sat in jail until his bail was paid off according to how much it cost a day to sit in jail. I believe in the Bible scripture "Train up a child the way he should go, and when he is older, he will not depart from it." A lot of people are not too particular about public defenders because they seemed like they are not really in your corner. Sometimes, he seemed like he is and other times, he seemed like he's not. I don't know the behind the scenes when he talked with the prosecutor. We do know this for sure they do not want to let it go. It's a night mare for me and my family. I think about the times when he was a little boy, and I would be so stressed out from my past job. I sometimes would pick up take at food for dinner for Joey and his sisters, and then go straight, to my room to laid down, after a stressful day at work due to being harassed at work. Joey would come to my room and bring me some of the dinner. Some of the staff were picking on me, one person poured coffee on my boots, and at the same time, several of the staff including him were trying to hit on me, and it was all unwanted. One day, I came back from vacation, and one of them got fired because his harassment was so severe to me. They fired him after everything was calmed down, and on top of that, he was married.

CHAPTER

6

I LEARNED TO ALWAYS KEEP YOUR resumes going. I also read to also try to go on a job interview.

I hope that my son will be okay and learn from this terrible experience. We've been back and forth to court, and my full-time job required me to sometimes as the last resort to go to court. I do not like going to court. So far, my son's case had not gone to trial. He grew up in the church, went to private religious schools, but all that and talking about doing his best to stay from under the law enforce radar. He has been pulled over a couple of times. Not sure what prompted that, but from what I see, it's really tough out here. I am saying I am not sure because my son was saying that he did not do anything wrong. It was a blessing for us that the state trooper brought him home, and I had to walk to get our vehicle. I was going to catch the bus, but the bus blew straight pass me. I am just waving to flag the driver down, and I was at the bus stop. I hope this book inspires others to not get swept up in the world of confusion but to fight back with the strength and will to move on and to be the best you can be. Always try to set an example when possible. Yes, I made some mistakes, but I took in the good, the bad and the ugly, and I learned from the bad and the ugly, and I appreciate the good always. Sometimes, I do not like to say this, but not everyone's family is family. It is a blessing to have relatives that treat you well. Sometimes, it is hard to try to explain when you are distant from your family when you are speaking with someone who is close-knit to theirs. I always wanted to be close-knit to all my relatives, but some of them were so mean and flat-out abusive; it was so hard to tell my children. I tried but nobody deserves to be hurt or killed or tortured by the hands of a stranger or the hands of family that's not acceptable either.

I read in a book when I said to myself I wanted to break this vicious cycle that me and my siblings went through. This book said, "If a person do not treat you right, they will not treat your children right." I do believe that, and I already had made up in my mind that I would change it. I love people, and children trust their family. Sometimes, adults make mistakes by leaving their children with the wrong family members. How do you know? Or if something is said like the time my great-great aunt in New York knew that one of the cousins liked me who lived in California in an unnatural way, where did this come from? If she knew, surely my mom knew. People say the past is the past. More and more people these days even celebrities have stepped forward and said they have been abused. I commend them because I have learned that it is not just something that you blew off and grew out of; abuse is something that if you make it through, it's something that you survive. It takes courage to say you have been abuse or mistreated by a family member. Like my mother said she left her children with family she said "but they are family". I wanted better for my children, I wanted to break the cycle of abuse and not to leave my children here there and everywhere, just to have a good time. I knew I wanted better than I had growing up. I knew I wanted my children my children to be able to slept well, without being afraid of some family member or baby sitter hopping in the bed with them. I was blessed that when we moved from a two-bedroom apartment of 11 years to a four-bedroom house. Each of my children were able to have their bedroom. I did what I could to make sure my children had their own space. Here's the strangest part; there were other abusers in the family. I lived with my great-great auntie, and my uncle lived there too in the day. He was long ago a heroin addict and got help, but I could say this he never abused me in no shape, form or fashion. He was always there to help my great auntie; my mother wasn't around a lot. He always had a good time with my mom, and I never seen them, argue. The only time I saw them have a difference in opinion was when my great-great aunt passed away. For some reason, my mother's lived in boyfriend who came to town but could not stay for the funeral. I took the Grey hound bus to New York right away during final exam times from college. So, I had money to get there; it was a very long bus ride. Mother only had enough money to get me back to school. My mom had her good moments I told her that she could use the money to get back to California on the bus. My father paid my way back. Sometimes, I wonder what happened to her. Is it because my dreams were on the sideline because getting together with my ex, she was not too particular about him. She always gave me a difficulty, maybe because we were so opposite from each other. She used to call me plain Jane. It was as if she had mixed feelings for me ever since I was a child. It was like do I like my kid or not? There were other situations regarding how she treated the other siblings, but this story is about me, Sophie the girl with the will and dreams to survive and Sophie the woman with the will and dreams to survive. Do not ever let anyone tell you that you are too old to follow your dreams. Thanksgiving is coming up, I just hope and pray that I can have a Thanksgiving dinner with all of my children. I used to invite people over, but everyone is doing their own thing now. This year, I want all the fiddles to be made the day before. Even when our family was invited out to dinner, I would cook the Thanksgiving dinner, my father would laugh when I would call him and let him know. Sometimes, the littlest glimpse of happiness, even the thought of happiness, is a real pick me up. There is so much in life to always fight for. Goals are so important in life.

Even the smallest goal can turn out to be the biggest milestone. For example, it seemed like I am taking far too long to crank out this book. Let the truth be told five years ago, I was not thinking about writing a book. I always enjoyed giving great advice to others, and finally, someone told me if I follow my own advice that I give to others; I will be alright. It always seemed like I am trying to reach a goal trying to be in love with someone, but it would be like yet so close but so far away. For some reason, love had been a hard thing for me to hang on, but you know what I must have been hanging on to the type of love that was just not meant for me to have. Even at my age, my children are all grown-up now, and I have not given up on love.

So I decided to take advantage of my singleness turning my loneliness and despair of the thought of wanting to be in love but haven't gotten that cup of coffee or in my case a cup of tea I turned it around. I turned loneliness into busyness and not turning despair into desperation, but looking at it as me time. There is so much unhappiness that seemed like if you let it, it will consume one. Sometimes, there are days that you admire others when you think all is good with them. They say it's tough basically, but I am fighting. If you fight to get better, in my opinion, it gets better. One day, I was in the grocery store, I've been working one of those seven-day straight full times for a couple of weeks in a row. I dragged myself into the grocery store; my feet were hurting me so bad. As I walk down the grocery aisle, there was a woman much younger than me who appeared to be in a lot of back pain. It seemed like it was truly a great burden to be in the store shopping because she was in so much pain. After I've seen this young woman, I forgot about my feet, which were no longer hurting anymore, I no longer felt tired. I realized at that very moment my sore feet weren't as bad as having to stand and your back was in so much pain. As she stood next to the line, I was in the next line over and could hear her softly groaning from pain. I asked her if she would like to step over to the line I was in because I was the very next person in this line to check out, but she could go next. The brief movement we stood while we were in line, she was telling me her back was in a lot of pain, and she herself just got off from work. She was also telling me that she has a small child who was in the hospital, and that she also had to go to the hospital to see her. Her child had to have surgery. I hope that all's well with her family. I pray that everything's well with the woman and her child.

I remember too well what's it like to have a young child in the hospital.

I sometimes can be so comfortable in doing something, which can become routine and where you still feel the same way years down the line, sometimes you end up walking away in the long run. I really need to go ahead and finish this book. Because maybe I can inspire others. I want to inspire myself to get moving even when negativity seems to be wearing me down in the surroundings I am in. I have been working sometimes seven days a week. I need to get back to the gym. I was going to the gym faithfully.

I saw these commercials about dancing into shape. It's funny when I was in my twenties, I was not a faithful gym goer, and when I decided to go, I did not go for long. I enjoyed dancing and most of the time I stayed slender. Although I do think regular exercise is very healthy. Never let sorrow consume you. You got to keep it moving. Sometimes, you can be so successful with helping people, the same people you are helping will turn on you, or when they are thinking to have someone to replace you, they will and get rude with you. Not all the time this will happen. Maybe someone can relate to what I am saying. Sometimes, you just got to know when to roll out. I realize that this could be a mistake.

I remember in New York I was so unhappy with how the stresses of school were going for me. The back and forth transferring can never be good for any child. I was bouncing back and forth from California to New York so much as a child. The same children I remember from elementary school in New York, I would not see them again until junior high; then I am taken out again and back to school in California. This went on so much that one day in California High School, I was called down to the school office. The high school in New York contacted the high school in California to tell them I was still in enrolled in their school. Now that I am an adult, I found that a little odd, but maybe not. The school probably was concerned about my well-being and to make sure that I was okay. The person in the office said technically she was supposed to send me back there. I think maybe she was just trying to scare me. It was not even no better when she asked me for my phone number, my mom changed her number a lot and still do, we just got a new number. It just so happen I have the number with me, and I opened the piece of paper and read the number to her. How did the school in New York know I was back in California going to school? I was back in New York going to high school, and my close friend Tangy was no longer my close friend. I was snatched away from them, and in that crowded hall, we just shuffled past one another, and several other friends I remember from elementary and junior high school, that showed that their environment was stable. My mother had the nerve to say I had my three children, and it's not good to transfer them around from different day cares. If I see trouble at a day care, then why would I keep my child there, or using sticks or the type of wood chips used for landscaping. in a sand box instead of sand? I wanted nothing more than a stable environment for my children. In my adult life, so far I only moved three times, two apartments and a house. My children, while growing up, lived in an apartment and then to a house. You never know how much you have until you are ready to move. I did not load a medium-moving truck, but we used one large truck and put everything in that one truck. Came back got up the residue, and it was hard looking back at an apartment that you stayed for eleven years, but having happy moments too. Eventually, we found a day care that my children liked and me too. It's okay to pop in to visit the day care or go sit down and have breakfast with your child at day care. When you choose a day care, it is an important decision to make. I recently had my birthday. I washed cars on my birthday because I needed money. This was a temporary job that I kept on saying: this may be my last day due to the weather. I went to college thinking that what was going to happen may open the roads to success.

Sometimes it's difficult because I always wanted to be the best I could be. Even though I was being abused as a child and people in my own family tried to break me, I am still the person that I was meant to be. All I ever wanted to do was to help and be there for someone, but if for some reason that could no longer be, people will change. I learned that everyone didn't want to be your friend even if you were very kind to them. I never forget when my mom moved us from New York into the intercity of California; she could only afford to live in some real tough places. No grass in front of the building, and the landlord had no desire to plant any. I bet the landlord had grass in their yard. My mother did not get child support. When my parents stopped speaking, they stopped speaking. My father could lose his temper on us. My mother would defend us. I'm sorry to say, but I think spankings inflict so much pain on the body; and if you have a child who just does his own thing, it will not change it. I will never forget the same year I graduated from high school. Our apartment building was being condemned. I was also going to be staying on campus also. Well, anyway, I was laying down on the couch in our living room, and our living room windows were open. As I laid on the couch, I was so surprised what was being said outside under my family's living room: one of the other children, they name everyone in my household, stated we were all going to be living in a dog house, because we had nowhere to go. I played it off immediately after she made that comment. I looked out the window at the time I was still a child myself, and I just politely said hello to her, and the other child was looking at her expressing what she had on her face was priceless. I just wanted to acknowledge that one of the people whom she predicted the future heard their fate (laughing out loud). There have been so much going on in the world. It seemed like the world is going backwards. There was so much racism in the world. A lot of people are just plain afraid of the police. Recently, my son and I were going to the license bureau, and a policeman jumped over three lanes to follow us. We were in a mostly white area. I was so nervous. My son did not know he was following us. I pulled in a parking spot, and the officer remained parked in a police car in the parking lot. I got out of the car but left the car door open to look at the time because the license bureau was closed due to the holiday. As I was walking back to my car, the officer said to me, "The license bureau close, uh?" It was very fortunate for me that I had another day to get my car registration renewed. I did not know what made him follow us. Was it because of the color of our skin or the type of car I was driving with personalized plates or a combination of both? I was just glad that no harm came to us due to people not wanting to let the centuries of the past go. I feel that all people should be treated equally. I do my very best to treat people the way I would like to be treated. If everyone treated people in a positive manner and treated people the way human beings ought to be treated, I truly believe the world would be a better place. As I write this book, I must admit I am a very lonely person.

I believe that no matter how old you are, everyone deserves to continue to enjoy life. I have not been on a date in years. I have had men do a little flirting, but nothing real like if you are interested, let me know. I may just be interested in them. I know I can get a date or a man, but I just do not want anyone. It goes for men to just do not settle because what you settle for you may regret. I am so bad with meeting Mr. Right. I just wonder is it because I have not been taught any better or have not seen a lot of successful relationship in my own family? I am grown-up now, but I am no spring chicken. I do know that the word loneliness is a lonely word. I admire people who come out and say that they are lonely because that takes a lot of courage. Sometimes, people work so hard to maintain, such as myself that I hardly go anywhere to meet anyone. I've been out of the dating game for so long. I just have accepted the fact that I may not be meeting anyone. I just have to see. As the year came to an end, there was so much going on in my own family. My son Joey was having some problems. When something happens in life to a young person, the society wants to blame it on three things: either the color of the skin, the upbringing, or not having good role models. We are so convinced that these are the reasons. It is not for me to say. I have made some very poor mistakes in life, but I have always tried to help my children. I have my oldest daughter Leah who is past twenty-five years old and lives with me, and she always blames everything on me. It takes two people to make a baby, but most of the time, the mother is always blamed when something goes wrong, as far as I can see. They say jobs are hard to fine, but some are able to bounce from one job to the next, and others are having a tough time.

It is best to get all the education that one can get. I remember when I was going on college visits in high school, the students had to pay their own way. Now to my understanding, the student can get assistance. When my baby girl Vonya went to visit the college she graduated from, they sent her a round- trip airplane ticket to visit. The only problem she had was in Washington where they thought the plane had left, but it didn't. That was scary to us both I thought I was going to have to go to Washington to get her. I had not been to Washington. I want to go, but every time I plan the trip with a tour guide, either it is booked, or I have to work. I have been blessed for two out of my three children graduated from college. Joey is trying, but he is facing an uphill battle. He has not been in church for a while. I have not been in several months, but Joey has not been in years. I always tell him that we should go to church together. I have been working on Sundays not making much, but it helps. Making about $122 after taxes. I have an education and is struggling. I thought it was because of my age, but people older than me change jobs and get paid very well.

You can do your best to raise up a child the way you think they ought to go. Now the words "the way you think they ought to go." Most parents always want the best, but what if the child just stays in a bad situation? I have always tried to help my son Joey. Most of the time, he didn't listen to what I say. Then the minute he gets into a jam, he calls on me. My children's father and I do not get along. For some reason, he does not respect me. One time he said I was ugly, but I am not. Once, he said he was better than me. I have never known him to truly provide for his children. He has another set of children as well. Unfortunately, he had a drug and alcohol problem, which once I had to call the emergency to get him to the doctor because he was just not himself anymore. I had to fight a battle within myself that I was not going to allow him to destroy my life. Once he went into the hospital that night, it seemed to make him a little better. He was no match for me. Still he was my children's father, and they do love him, just like I love mine. Sometimes, one has to wake up mentally and realize it's time to move on and do not depend on a person who has always cheated on you and never married you after numerous promises. I am saying these things in my book because low self-esteem and self-pity will really bring you down. There is something going on with me right now, maybe someone else out there has experienced the same thing; it is called unfinished business.

If I finish all my unfinished business, maybe it will be okay. I always wanted to play the piano. Some of my unfinished business is learning how to play the piano, finish getting my real estate license and get my master's degree in public administration.

You want to be careful what kind of major you choose. I chose fashion merchandising, but for some reason, it did not get me past sales. I was once a manager trainee in a shoe department, but I had to quit because my baby's father was not properly assisting with our firstborn and was dropping her off with other women to care for. How I know he was dropping her off because these women were coming to me and telling me so. Yes, my life had been one big nightmare, maybe I only had myself to blame because of the type of man I had chosen. I can say I was never on drugs or have done alcohol, even if he had tried to coach me to do so. I was just hanging on to my goals and dreams. Beating the odds was a stepping stone to the possibilities of my life. I never knew why my dreams and goals seemed so far away. I do know that some people who once believed in God stopped believing in God. I never stopped believing in God, and I feel his presence all the time. I remember when I was a child, I was very ill, but I still got down on my knees and prayed to God. Recently, I heard my children's father say that he did not believe in God. It did not surprise me at all. He was over five years older than me. I was in my car along with our son. We have to take care of business with regard to my son. A father's words have such a strong meaning to their sons. I looked at one of his friends as a child was always in trouble. His father sent for him from another state to take care of him. I would hear him say to his son, "I love you." He was there to ground him when he was wrong. That same trouble child is now a productive adult. He finished high school, had a really good job and was back in the state where his mother lived. From time to time, he came back to California to visit his father and my son. When it comes to raising a man and the father is available, they should try to guide them in the right direction.

I do believe in the Bible verse that says, "Train up a child in the way he should go and when he is older, he will never depart from it." I believe in that Bible verse. I know my son was brought up in the church, and he got baptized. I know he will learn to listen and not to wait to the too-late minute. You must pick and choose your friends wisely especially in relationships. I know my life is not perfect, and I never claimed it to be. Sometimes, people will tend to judge you without knowing anything about you. Again, I hope this book will have inspired someone out there so much to understand. As long as you can, you can make a difference in your life and of someone's life.

This weekend, I did not have to work at the rental carwash; they did not need the help. The temp agency always sends five to six people. I hope this time to use my time, I have to get back into my healthy habits such as piano lessons and exercise classes because right now, my soul is crying tears. It seems like everything I have tried to do I feel like I am running on a treadmill. Success is more than the money that a person makes. To me, all your children are staying out of trouble. They say there is one in every family that should be embraced and find out what's causing it to be the root of the problem. When your ex tells you he's better than you, but he can't pay for your son's hair- cut, let him talk. He wants you to feel bad you did not allow to let him continue to wear on your nerves, so he wants to make you feel bad. Do not let him or her do it; move on with your life. Success to me is moving on from things, and people who have done damage to your life, it's not about who always has the sharpest outfit, who has the longest hair, or who is the best looking or drives the sharpest car, but it's about your inner being and your happiness being around the ones that love you and being around the ones you love back. People tell me that I am losing weight, but I am not exercising. If people are not treating you right, it's time to move on even if it's your own family (sad to say). There are so many domestic violence cases out there. I have been blessed to not have to call off an entire day for sick time. Sometimes, it is not good because you may end up getting ill on your way in. I have not vomited in a while, but I used to order this frozen food. One of my children said it may have been due to the food, but no one else got sick. It could have been the stress that I was under. One time I got news about something, and I knew I was not prepared, and my stomach got so upset I started throwing up. As I write this book, I have not worked on it in a while. So much was going on in my life. I was struggling to pull myself out of this funk that I am in. It felt like things are crashing down on me.

My son was in jail, and as I visited him, I've never seen so many black young men in jail. I believe my son did not know how to pick his friends. I tried to teach my son to live a peaceful and productive life. Some nights I couldn't sleep knowing he's in jail. I visited him once a week. Visiting hours are during the week in the afternoon and early in the morning on the other day before noon. We cannot even afford a lawyer; we had to get a public defender who he is not giving the impression that he is in Joey's corner at all. He has even gotten smart with me. He said to me if I wanted him out, I would get a bail bonds- man. I told him if I had the money for a bail bondsman, my son would be out. This situation had been going on for several months until Joey was out on bond. First, I only have to pay down about 374. For a 2,500, he got it arraigned, and it became ten thousand bond; soon I did not have the money, so we put our home up. One day, he was told by the public defender the other accusations were made about him and was told to meet with the judge the next busi- ness day. Well, Joey never missed an appointment. We went there, the lawyer was late. I went to put some money on the meter, and Joey was arrested and his bond revoke. He had been in jail; the bond now's too high for me. We have been asking for a bond reduction. I hope it can be lowered. I hope this would be over soon, and Joey can come home. Once a person started putting up a property, especially their home, in which they actual live in, money is tight. It's like all these crazy and disturbing accusation, I don't believe it to the point one of the accuser tried to drag me in it. I believe in what was in the Bible that says, "Train up a child the way he should go, and when he is older, he will never depart from it." I just kept saying that verse in my head over and over again. I told Joey to choose his friends wisely; the same person who he thought was his friend turned on him. Joey was brought up in the church, and he was saying he did not believe in God. I got a letter from him since he had been in jail saying that he's been praying and how he has been reading the Bible. My prayer has been answered he even talked about going to church with me again. I heard his father say that he did not believe in God either. I remember he would go to church, so what happened to make my children's father an unbeliever. His father was there and told me he was arrested in the justice center while we think he was going to meet with the judge. I told Joey that being out on bond is a time to get himself in order and prove his case. I told him this as a mother who is fighting for her son's freedom, with nothing more than a prayer and no financial money to even hire a lawyer who will fight for my son's life. I told him to take care of himself and choose his friends wisely. This was a critical time for the family. Even though I lived in a low-income neighborhood, I always strived for my family to do well. We struggled to hang on to the house we leased with an option to buy. I was supposed to at least stay there for two years and then buy, but my credit was not the best, and I really did not know how to go about purchasing the home; the manager of the house was giving me such a hard time about it. There were a couple of issues we had with the housing while we were leasing it from the guru housing firm. Once the gas pipe from the furnace was leaking, and we did not notice, one day, a family member came over, who is a scientist, and said that he smelled gas. No one smelled it but him. I remember my stomach started hurting all the time, and it was getting worse, but the children showed no visible symptoms. The maintenance team came out and brought a contractor and said we were blessed to be alive. I know I was having trouble sleeping. I felt like I was heavily drugged but could not sleep. I managed to get to the phone and call the gas company and 911, but I felt myself slurring as I spoke. I got the children up, and we waited in the car with the windows down. The gas company confirmed it was a gas leak from the pipe. They turned the gas off. The children were in elementary school, and I think Joey was not going to school yet, but in child care. Years down the road in my home, I still could not afford to purchase the house. A couple of years later the carbon monoxide detector that went off. I called the fire department, and they confirmed that it was carbon monoxide coming from the stove. Our lives were spared by God. The maintenance person came in the day and installed a new stove. Shortly after that, I was informed that the owner placed me in a program where I could finally be able to purchase the home, and I become a homeowner. I'll never forget I could get put out from the home because they could not find my rent or either I had trouble financing the home. I was glad the rent was found, and I own the home. One day, if I move, I want to live in another state, but I hope and pray that Joey will win this case and will come home. When everything is okay, we can relocate. I hope both of my daughters want to come too; if they are married, maybe we'll all come. I do not want to relocate unless my son is released from jail and is able to relocate too. Hope he will be released soon. When I write this book, I have some other things to bring to the forefront. It's so hard for me to go on a date, especially since my family is having difficulty with what's going on with Joey. It's like my life is on a stand-still. I am not going to allow the odds to slow me down. There are so many times, I believe in the power of prayer and to each his own. I pray that my only son, my youngest, can come out of this terrible situation and move on with his life. It seems like so many young men especially black men are in jail. When I stand in line to see him there are mostly black people in line. The lines can be really long at times. I never thought in a million years that I would be going to visit my son in jail. I sent him to private schools all his childhood. I hope this book will also be a learning tool that no matter how you try to live your life or raise your family, situations can come up. He reminds me in his letters to work on my book. Goals are so important.

CHAPTER

7

THE REASON GOALS ARE SO important is because each day I am allowed to wake up, I truly believe that I could be a better person than I was yesterday. Before I started working on this book, I thought that I should be doing a lot better than I should. Sometimes, it is easily said than done. In life, sometimes you have to work very hard to get what you want. Be careful with job interviews; what I have experienced not all but some ask questions, do not assume. I know whenever I assume, it becomes disastrous.

Some examples of it's okay what type of job interview you are on. I saw an ad about an assistant store manager at a major department store. I got to the interview, and I learned to ask questions. I asked, "Was this in regard to the assistant store manager position?" I was told no, a part-time sales positions. I did not accept the position even though I was receiving unemployment; it would not have benefitted me or my family to accept the position. Another case, my unemployment was running low, so the upscale department store again was looking for an assistant store manager, but this time closer to home, and my unemployment was about to end in one week. This time, it got worse. I did not know that I was speaking with the newly appointed assistant store manager. He told me to come in and be interviewed for the position. When I got there, he did not interview me; but when I asked the person if I was interviewed for the assistant manager position, I was told no, but a part-time position. This time, I had no choice but to accept the position and work the job with grace and charm until I found a full-time job. Eventually I did, and I put in a two weeks' notice. The next example when I knew I heard the interviewer over the phone that I would be making $40,000 a year, and at the time I was unemployed, but my offer letter stated $14 per hour, which is about $29,000 only a year. I took it because I did not have a choice. I had a couple more situation with misleading job ads. Questions are important, so ask at a job interview.

I spoke about Joey's plight with law. It is so hard on the family; Joey is truly missed. Right now, as I write the book, on my side of the family, his sisters and myself offer him support. Now as Joey is in jail, they are trying to raise his bond triple the amount; this is all because of hanging with the wrong person who was supposed to be a friend. Only God knows the truth and whoever was involved. When blacks are caught up in the system, they truly don't want to let them go. I go once a week to see him. The hours are terrible during the afternoon and during the week. I know that workdays are tough. I tried to get on the same schedule to see him every week, so my job would not start giving me a hard time. I only go to see him once a week. This is the time I wish I had finished all my goals. If I had finished all my goals, I could have gotten a lawyer who'll fight and go hard for Joey. I asked and prayed that God be his attorney. I believe in doing a job to do it to the best you can. Lately, on the first part of the year, someone was coming in my driveway in the wee hours of the morning and had started putting small damages on my sports car. Now I had to start turning my porch light on again at night. I have had this convertible for a little over a year. I have never had to cut on my porch light because someone was vandalizing my car. So far, it has stopped. I hope it does not happen again. It's good to get a road hazard or insurance on your tires. Tonight, I had two tires that were low; one was really low. I hope that no one tried to bother my tires too because I do not bother nobody. Just as I thought it could not get any worse, I found out today, my water got turned off in the middle of the winter. I just did not have the money to pay for it and was going to once I got my income tax. I got a lot of bottled water. I am going to get up and be at the water department to see what I can work out. I remember a while back that once a year, you could get a break, and they would not cut your water off. Now since the water was off, no one was here. Joey stayed and went over to his dad's house and went somewhere to take a shower. This was the third time in twenty-year time frame that I had my water off. Twice one summer. Once it was off back on, I did not have a job. When my income tax check came in, I paid something on it, and they turned it back on. That same summer, I did not have a job and came back from a job interview, and the water was turned off again. If I had finished my goals or not have been intimated about high goals, my water would be on. I know that this will not happen again. I have three goals to accomplish.

Ever since I was a child, I would feel this void in my life that I was born to do something great. I learned this spirit is part of what God has for me. I truly believe that God has a plan for me, and my age in this case is nothing but a number. Maybe my greatness is to make a difference in people's lives, especially when you are working with the public. Being humble is a good thing but have confidence in yourself. I remember when my kids were younger; no one really came around to visit us, and I read in a book that "if a person don't treat you right, they will not treat your children right." I believe that too. Anyone who did not treat me right whether when I was a child or an adult, those same folks either rarely on their own came in contact with me or my children. Then they wondered why we do not come around; my children asked why I did not allow them around certain family members. It's nothing personal; it's just business. I tried to be kind to everyone, but I did not want to subject my children to any-one no matter who that are mean and abusive to me. I should have spoken out about it. I understand that I did not have that support to speak out about abuse, as a child without backlash out about it. Once my mother's live-in boyfriend tried to hit on me, I never forgot it. It was check and food stamp my mother went to the grocery store, and I was in my room listening to some music. I was about fifteen years old, and I was still a virgin. I was in my room listening to my forty-five records. Then he came in the doorway and sat on my bed. At that point, he said all girls want to be initiated, and that he tried to put his arms around me. I turned off my music and ran out of my room. I ran to the back door, and he had the chain on the door; it so happened my mother came back from the grocery store. He was such an abusive person; he would beat my mom all the time. If she looked too good, he would beat her, threatened to knock my teeth out. He hit one of my brothers when he was about four in the chest with his fist; all that ruckus and nights he lived with us until my freshman year of college.

I can say Joey has inspired me to go ahead and finish this book. I hope when it's about time I finish creating this book, he will be a free young man. There are so many dating websites and a lot of different ways to meet that special someone. I see a couple of people trying to get in touch with me over the Internet. I do not want to meet anyone from online; it could be dangerous, and they may not be who they say they are. Sometimes if you meet somebody that you did not meet online, you still have to do your due diligence; there are free websites that one can do a background and credit check. There are people who have much success in online dating. To be honest right now, I am not ready to date.

My plate is so full of family concerns. I just want to work on a better life. What I want right now is my son to be a free man and my water to be turned back on. I wonder what the water department will say. I know for lights and gas, if you have medical approval, they will turn it back on. I did not even get a ten-day notice. I should have filed rapid refund, but it would take out so much money. I definitely did not see this one coming. My dad told me something about cars being repossessed because that happened to me a couple of times; that is "when you are behind, they can take your car at any time." Again, I want to say I hope my story will encourage someone because even though I am in a situation, I pray and believe that God will make a way. Sometimes, I wonder how a situation could have taken a turn for the worse. It's one of the coldest month of the year, and I am still without water. I have been without water for three weeks, and it feels longer than that. I feel like a camper boiling everything. The restroom situation can be tough, but I have a system for that. I want to be kind to everyone I meet. You never know who is in a dire strait situation. Disconnect utility bills, and Joey is still in jail. It's tough for him in there he never had a prior record. I tried so hard to raise him to continue to do his best and stay out of trouble. These days, it can be difficult to not to be caught in some type of situation with the wrong people and not listening to the people who love him. It is such a hard pill to swallow right now. I hope and pray he can come home soon. Every time I went to see him, I wished I could see him on both of the days. He could have visitors. The hours are tough if you work days. I write to him once a week and go see him once a week. He also writes back too. He started writing us first. I have been trying to find another job, but so far, I have not found one. If I have done my goals years ago in regard to making money, I could have afford to get Joey out on bond. Now the bond went to $50,000 and an additional $250,000. Plus, the $2,500 and then the $10,000 bond from the beginning. I didn't have $30,000 to get him out. I listened to someone speak about procrastinating. Procrastinating and excuses can go hand in hand. I knew I had to create a new way of thinking. Why spend so much time dwelling on the negative? Flip it and spend the time thinking about the positive. Instead of thinking what if it does not go right, then what? Let's flip that phrase. This sounds much better: What if this goes right, then what? There are so many successful. people who had a long road to success. It takes a lot of determination and drive to be successful and stay successful in life, and that it should be a way of life. Tomorrow is a promise to no one. Make every day count, and remember, there is a light at the end of tunnel.

You can only see the light if you keep traveling in the right direction of the light. Carrying the torch to see through the darkness of despair. It's getting difficult for Joey in jail now, and it's difficult for me. I always thought that Joey would not be in this situation. Every time I go see him, it's a mother's pain that only a mother who is in this situation would understand. We do not know his fate, only God knows. My daughter talked about this website; there are so many interesting people on this website, but one has to be so careful. I have not been on a date yet. Some games may be played too. I hesitated a little. One advantage online is you do not have to meet anyone you do not want to. There is also a new text free program, not that I am promoting online dating, if I can meet someone in everyday life, that would be a blessing. A lot of times I find myself hanging by myself. Sometimes, I would like to go out on a date night. With Joey in jail, it was like I put my life on hold. Some days it is really hard for me to wrap my mind about what has happened to Joey and my family. Once a young black man is caught in the system, it's so hard to get out. I know I have to be strong for people who depended on me and strong for myself. I know I am a child of God, and I have to keep telling myself this that Joey will be home soon. Sometimes, I go see him, and I wonder if he was saying positive things that he will be home soon because he believes that or he see how worn and beat down I look. People tell me that I am losing weight. I am also battling some other issues with some folks. It's like I am going to keep on believing there is a God. He's been with me for so long; he saved my life so many times. I learned you have to be careful in everything you do. I mean down to choosing your home church. Be cautious in everything. I think Joey is like me; we both learned the hard way. I would think that everyone was my friend, my very friend turned on me. I started having some problems in high school. One day, one of my little brothers said to me, "Sophie, there are two types of people in the world: us and them." Choose your friends wisely, be alone than hanging with the wrong people in my opinion. Joey has a smile that lights up the world. He thought that everyone is his friend. Now we are having a nightmare. We all have to "surround ourselves with people who are going to lift us higher." As I write this book, I do not bother people to make them feel bad or try to belittle anyone to make myself feel better; it is too much of that going on in the world. If we come together with our talent, skills and yes, help those with financial woes, it would help. I hear so much "I got mine, so you got to get yours." Sometimes, I hear "nobody helped me, why should I help someone?" I'll be amazed when I hear that. It makes me think if life was so bad that one can become so frugal, that the person cannot help anyone who needs help. I know if I had a lot of money, Joey would be out on bond, and we would hire a good attorney. If I had followed my dream for some of my goals like getting my real estate license over fifteen years again, maybe I would have enough money to bail out Joey. I bailed him out the first two times. The situation was getting worse and worse. His father has always been critical on me we can't hold a civil conversation. I basically asked him to be civil for his son's sake. As long as you are able to get up and go about your day, considered it a gift no matter what.

When I was a child, I wanted to be an actress. Today at my age, I went to audition for arts. It said from three years old to adult. I went home from church, ate and went to the audition. My children have been in performing arts. One even took it in college. I told them we should go. She really is good. For some reasons, she thought I was just talking about it. The audition was here for a couple of days. When I got there in the beginning, it was not crowded like I thought it would be so crowded, so I got there a little after it started. I almost ran out of the room I knew before I went there that I was probably too old. They should have had an age limit. The interviewer's look on his face was priceless (laughing). I really wanted my daughter to come to. She would really have a chance. She has taught theatre and was able to lead in several plays. The interviewer was nice. He said he did not scout the people in my age group, but they have a sister agency in Los Angeles, and he asked me if I would be interested. I said yes. Well, I do not think they will call. I see older people in the movies and as extras all the time. People kept on telling me I look like a famous actress. Maybe the interviewer saw something in me to forward me to the old folks' divisions, we shall see. I think with children, they should be kinder with letting them know if they have work for them. During this interview, the interviewer was very polite to everyone. The children are the most important that the interview should be done with class. I remember I took my children to auditions and they would not take Joey (due to the agency was not looking for younger males). The modeling agency just had no tack of it. I saw the look on my son's face.

Of course when you do not have the money, it is only wishful thinking. My mind as a child had been basically beaten to dust. I became shy in public sometimes. I remember doing a play, just a small part, but a part of me still had that will to succeed despite the abuse I endured. I remember being in a fashion show. I never understood why my mother was always so late for school activity that was so important to me; it was really odd. In Oakland, she was like a different parent like she did not care. In New York where Aunt Rose lived in my hometown, she acted like she cared. She would read us stories, buy us nice clothing, but we still got painful spankings. I am not faulting my mother for her troubles. Her mother died when she was young; I never met her. I was told she was very smart and graduated from high school at the age of sixteen years old. I would take my mother shopping to buy her some gifts. When she was at a good mood, she would buy me clothing too. Some said she got upset at me because she felt the children father was not my soul mate. I had thought if I stopped the relationship with him, my life would get better. So, I did, and my life did get better, and I even felt better. The children did not understand, why their parents did not stay together. When I was a teenager mother would either have missed the school, programs or late. For my college graduation I know the family was not there for the ceremony because I heard no clapping when I walk across the stage. Come to find out that Mother and Uncle Leon came from New York (he was alive then) and other family members were there. I was told by Uncle Leon that Mother wanted to go get something to eat and when they got back I saw them in the empty parking lot that an hour ago was once filled with cars. I gave my mother my college degree diploma and I never saw it again. Mom never hung it on her wall, nor did she know where it was. I have not been to church in a while. I went to visit a church today. Yesterday, I got out to get some fresh air. After, what has happened to Joey, I stayed home getting rest on the weekend. I also put in a lot of extra hours at work. Saturdays have been my leisure days. I felt better just getting out. My children have been my inspiration, but before they were born, my inspiration was just doing what I wanted to do in life. I was going to relocate back to New York, but once I started living on my own, my life was a lot more peaceful. I want to relocate now, but as long as Joey is incarcerated, I do not want to leave the area. I want to be able to see him on a regular basis. I am concerned about him in there.

"Life sometimes can be hard for no reason at all." I have bills all over the place. I have to choose between water and property taxes. Phone service or car note. I pray every day for my lights not to get cut off. The decisions that people make are depending on the need, depending on an individual need. My light bill was due yesterday. I thank God that my lights are still on. Sometimes, I wonder why life have been so tough on some folks. Sometimes, when I know I am not making enough money to even have me living comfortable, if I keep trying, there will be a better and brighter day. I pray every day and truly believe that everything is going to be okay. I work so hard for everything I get, and I want to fight to keep it. Staying focused is the key. If I had been focused on my goals, I would have reached them by now. Funny my water is off, and the news is talking about how the water department made a big mistake on water bills. The media talks about the meters not reading right, people water being shut off. What the water department told me was that my water was registered off since 2014. I have been getting water bills on a regular basis. The news just said that the water department are billing people for $40,000. and turning off the water. This is crazy. I was upset because my water was turned off. They did not work with you like the gas and light department. I hope that my lights will stay on until I get paid in two more days. The water department period need to stop being so harsh. The news says bills said the estimate, but there was a problem with that. No one should be afraid to go home in fear of no lights, gas, and not taken by surprise that you have no water. One person on the news was without water for three months. I picture myself in that type of situation. I hope and pray that I am spared with that type of situation. Right now, it's been almost one month since I had no water. Tonight, as I work on my book, I heard some noise like some-thing's rumbling around the house. I looked out the window, and there were unmarked police cars outside one of the neighbor's house again. There is an elder person living there too. One morning, I went out, and there were unmarked police cars everywhere for the neighbor family member. The same day Joey was home, he went to throw away the trash, and he said the officers started searching through our trash. Yes, "life can be hard for no reason at all." As I work on my story of my life, I can hear the winds howling in the wee hours of the morning. The lights flicker twice. Since I still do not have no water, it's been a month in two days. I thank God for the electricity and the gas and my home. I just fought so hard to keep this house even when I was a renter. I just heard a thump on the roof. Something must have blown on it. I hope and pray that everything is alright out there in the elements. Now I got something in the mail saying that if I do not pay my sewer, it will be turned over to the property taxes, but the water will remain off. When you are in a dilemma such as this, you must look at the bigger picture.

CHAPTER

8

I WEIGH MY OPTIONS. I DEFAULTED on my payment plan for the property taxes because I did not have the money for the current taxes, meanwhile back at the ranch, I still do not have running water. I am thinking what do I do? Now with the large amount of water bill and the sewer bill, my income tax check just would not cover it.

I thought to myself do I pay the property taxes or get my water turned on. I chose to pay the taxes. I said I will put myself on a pay plan until it gets done on my water and sewer bill. The thought process was what good would come out paying the bulk of two to the water departments. I was praying hard that the lights would not too be turned off. My prayers were answered. I ordered a beautiful green dress and a blouse. I did not think I would qualify for credit but would. I was shocked to get the dress on credit. It's such a pretty green. I look at it as a gift from GOD. It's very late I should be going to sleep. I was having a little trouble sleeping tonight, but I am a night owl. I do not want to be one tonight. Still, some people are damaging my cars right in my own driveway.

It's a shame I come home the other night, and the headlight of my other car that I do not even drive is broken. I hope and pray this would stop. I have never had this problem before. Hope this person is caught. It's so bad these days I do not put nothing past no one. Some knows that Joey is incarcerated. He's going through pretrial. I think he's getting a bad rap. What does a public defender do? I had to look it up because Joey's attorney seemed like he is defending the public because he ain't defending Joey as an attorney should. I pray that God will bring Joey home. I would like to go back to New York to visit when all of this is over. I wonder why it has always been so hard to find the right person for me. I am saying this because I have a crush or had a crush (sigh). He has been going through so much himself that he's probably in his own world. He has the most beautiful smile I have ever seen. He maybe even seeing someone. I will use my late great-auntie Rose's phrase time will tell. Now, time has told he's not interested, or he would have been knocking on my door. If he did, he would know it's so much more to me. I would like to have had a good meal and just talk with him. He is a private person I can tell. He has given the impression that he thinks that there's nothing special about me because the street I live on is supposed to be in the category worst street ever in California. I say this because he looked amazed when I told him what I do for a living, and he acted like the distance I had travel was nothing. I told him I traveled further than that to take my daughter across the country to attend a university in upstate New York, he grasped (I laughed out loud as I write this part). I hope on my next book writing, I have another miracle or gift to tell about what God gave me. I applied for some assistance with my water bill. The first time, I was turned down. I believe in a miracle every day, and that God will make a way out of no way. That is one of my favorite songs we sung when I was in the church choir, and it's the truth. I believe in a miracle from God daily. I know he can turn my world right side up. This has been a trying time. I have been receiving medical from the county department, and it ended the end of last year. I did not have to pay for it, but now, I have to pay for medical expenses. It's so expensive. A single parent with dependents cause me a little over $200 biweekly. I couldn't believe the prices to stay healthy are so expensive. For dependents, I am glad that the law has changed. To my understanding, the dependents that you used to have in college is up to twenty-six years of age. Now, the dependents just have to be only twenty-six years of age. However, dental is separate. Dental insurance is so important to have, so please do not skip. A beautiful healthy smile speaks volumes. I only had the medical card. I have been trying to find another job though it's a tough decision to make. Due to all the hard work and late hours I put in, but to be behind, all my bills and no water makes it no longer a difficult decision to make. I was thinking if something comes available at the job, I should apply for it. I pray that I can afford to go back to college to update my three classes out of four so I can pursue real estate. The struggle is real. I have not cried on the outside, but the inside of me find it hard to keep my soul's composure. I find music to be so smoothing. Right this very second, I am listening to the late great Isaac Hayes's rendition of "Walk on By." I have been off work for days now. This is the first time I have taken a vacation this year.

I have learned that taking the time out for yourself is the best thing in the world to do. You do not have to go on a vacation but just get away based on the time you have worked to get it. I learned to take a couple of days off every so often. I find it to be very relaxing, plus, I am not missed that much at work, and not so much wow, look what I got to do to get back on track because I take off one week or two in a row. I remember I had not been to a doctor in two years because I was dedicated to everyone and everything else. I got so sick. I did not know what was wrong with me. One moment I was fine, and the next, I got an allergic reaction and went into anaphylaxis shock. I went to two different hospitals. The first one was giving me pills and diagnosing me for the wrong illness. I finally went to another hospital, and they found out that I had asthma. I was not so surprised because a lot of people in my family has or had asthma. Asthma is a very serious illness and should be treated with care. In my home, we have cats. There's no air conditioner in the summer, which makes it very hard to breathe. Asthma is unpredictable you can think you are coughing, and it can be an asthma attack. One of my children also has asthma, and as a child, the doctor would not provide prescription medicine for the cold; they had to use the inhaler. I followed the child doctor's advice on myself as well. I still have my tea with my cough drop. There were times that I only had to get the refill just once a year. It was really important to keep an extra just in case I needed it and could not find the only inhaler. For the past couple of years since I've been having breathing troubles during bedtime and using the inhaler, a lot the doctor has changed my inhaler to another type and gave me some pill to take at night before bedtime. It's funny my first impression would not be able to get another chance. It's alright to change your doctors if something's not working for you even if it's down to personality differences. I only had to change a doctor due to attitude difference for me. Now the doctor that I have now. I was not too particular about personality, and I was going to change for the second time in a row. I noticed that every other doctor was booked up for at least a couple of months except for the doctor that I had (smile). I decided to give it one more shot and guess what? We got along great. We never exchanged words like the last doctor that I had. I was trying to avoid that situation, and I do not like confrontation because it's too draining and waste of my time. I often wonder what would change or happen to a person who go from believing in God to start not believing God. I notice that there are so many people who do not believe in God, and there are so many that do. My prayers have been answered to meet with the water department for a hearing to work with me to get my water restored.

When I am in trouble, I know I have to be very confident in how I present myself as a person. You cannot be afraid to defend yourself. My little sister once told me when she was a little girl and I in my teen's this: _ "Sophie, you are not afraid of anything." My answer to my little sister was sometimes, "I do be afraid sometimes but may not show it." Pray early in the morning as group helps. I got up for the 6:00 a.m. prayer line, and the prayer was strong. I would like to join the prayer line once a week.

I remember once I start watching this TV minster, and I would get prayer clothes in the mail, and I would make small donation as I recall, my children were very little. One day, I saw over the news that he was a fraud. I was so disappointed. At least it was out in the open. I know that not all pastors or evangelists on TV are frauds.

I went to the hearing about my extremely high water bill. It was tough. They informed me why the water was being shut off, but I never got a notice. They rarely work with people. They need to change their rules around. Flint, Michigan experienced crises and bad water leaving a lot of people access to no water. No one's water should ever be shut off. When some Detroit, Michigan residents water was shut off the media showed people being put in jail. One scene was a person in the wheel chair being put in the police truck for picketing. The head person at the hearing basically said we need water to live and we do. If the water department know that, then why won't they be better with working with people? I always thought if I had a lot of money, how I would help people? I remember a lot of times when I did not have not enough money, how I still helped others. There were times that the same people laughed at me when I was going through or flat being mean. I like to believe what goes around comes back around whether it's good or bad. There were times that I would say to myself no more begging to be someone's friend or trying too hard to be a person's friend or begging to hang on to a job, when you know you've made a difference, but it doesn't matter. I know I have to stay focused and continue to stay on my course of life.

Every day I wake up, I know I got to do my best. Every day I come home late from work. I admire how some people can leave on time, but not me. I always seemed to want to tie up some loose ends. Prayer works when after I was done with the 6:00 a.m. prayer phone line. I was happy all day. Even though I am going through terrible times. I hope this is a temporary storm that we are going through. I feel that God's presence is with us because things are getting better. I hope and pray that things get even better, and the release of Joey will happen soon.

There are times due to stress, I find it hard to sleep at night. I know that God is watching over me because he has brought me a mighty long way.

In church, the elders would say if I had a thousand tongues, that would not be enough to say thank you to GOD for being there through the bad and good. I truly tried to treat people the way I want to be treated.

I don't know everyone's story. Everyone's not going to write about their lives. Some people struggle all their lives trying to figure out why. Why to me is the most misunderstood word in the world. What I learned in the world I have a bad habit of wanting the wrong people to accept me. I will not call them negative people.

I do not like to use the term negative people because the same group of people or a person that is negative for me to be around maybe positive for someone else or fit in perfectly with another person. I remember my freshman year in college was so tough for me.

I was an inner- city child going to college with suburb children. I never had heard a couple of things; one was funny, and another was like wow. I was eating lunch with a group of students from the suburbs, and one young lady was eating lunch directly across from me. The student was very offended by a remark that there was debate that black children do not learn that fast unless they are talking about the children from the inner city. I thought to myself now to me, she is no different than the ones who made the negative remarks about our people as a whole race. All of a sudden, she asked me where I was from, and I yelled at her from Queens. She looked surprised. Sometimes, people are so quick to judge another person without stopping to question themselves. Are they somewhat clumping people together, according to a class as far as finances. I started to use a tape recorder to tape some of my thoughts because sometimes, I have that moment to capture an idea to put in the book, but later, I may forget. Actually, one thing that you know for a specific situation can be used for another. I never thought I would be using a tape recorder to write my book. There was a pretrial for Joey scheduled, and a hearing about my water. It's really something when you are in a disagreement with someone or something of authority, it's a battle. The bad press the water department is getting lately, it's in hopes that the water departments will be more like the electric and gas company, they will always try to work with you, and there are agencies that will actually pay a part of your bill. Some agencies will even apply something toward your bill every month. You can get medical certificates here for your lights and gas, but no real regular basic help. I am going to go on the 6:00 a.m. prayer meeting; it's worth getting up a little earlier. Sometimes, I think that no one's in my corner, but I look up, and GOD is there, God is real.

I would always take Joey to church and send him to private schools to avoid this type of situation being in jail. Even though all this is swirling around us, I always remember this Bible verse,- "Train a child up the way he should go, and when he is older, he will not depart from it." I always wanted the best for all my children. Sometimes, I beat myself up and say where did I fail, but I realized that's a mother's love, and it's not my fault. I regrouped myself and say despite the odds my other children finished college. Maybe there was not enough positive male role models for him. We exchanged Bible verses, and he even read one to me when meeting with him. I hope and pray that he can come home soon. I was informed that when a person is incarcerated, one can write a letter on his or her behalf. I am going to write a letter on behalf of Joey. So far, one letter was sent to the judge. Now three more are coming including one from Joey and one from me. Sometimes, it helps; and sometimes, it does not. People are so quick to judge. I wish that all people would not take into account how you look, but what's in your heart and soul.

There are a group of people that I do not see that much, but when I do see them, it's always sarcastic remarks and frowns. There are times that I say I am tired of begging for friends, and I am tired of begging period. Some people just have to take the time to learn to love, when hatred has taken them over. I am getting good news bit by bit, but I hope that the goods news adds up to solving the problems. No matter what happens, I believe God is good all the time.

I am grateful to be still in my home and have lights and gas. The heater has started to run cool. It's a lesson to make sure that every year you get your furnace check even though it has been running good in the past. I always have been getting my heater check, but this year, I had other pressing bills to pay. Every year I make sure that we have electric heaters to get in some heat. I should have included the maintenance of the furnace to be a pressing issue. Also, make sure that you have flashlight batteries, a flashlight and candles. I remember when power went out to the point I could not get gas from the gas station. Water was like gold. I got the last bottle of water in the convenience store; there lights were off. They were kind enough not to shut the store down because the times were truly turbulent. I really want to relocate.

I cannot relocate as my son is incarcerated. I have to be here so I can easily go and see Joey. I can see he wanted to come home; it's a real nightmare we want Joey to come home too. We want him to be free. I could not understand why some people won't be disturbed by other people who are having parties when people get out of jail quicker than a person who graduated with a degree. I get it's a matter of a person having their freedom. I know I should not be afraid. People are damaging my car in my driveway. I learn that God does not want his people to be afraid. It's something that the church I visited today basically spoke about. When you are a child of God, you should not be a slave to fear it was in a song, but it has truth to it. When I would be feeling down, I would keep in mind that others depend on me. My children love me. Most of all, God is good. I have people who depend on me. For example, when one goes to work, the employer depends on the employee to do their job acceptably and expect great things.

When I work for someone, I want to make them look their best and not their worst. It is also a reflection of my work ethics. When people think of you as an employee, it should be good thoughts and not an "oh, child please type of situation." I see a lot on social media where people are questioning the existence of God and the events that happened in the Bible. There are people that have grown-up on believing about God and his Son Jesus, and some are very successful in life. I do not understand why they change their minds and not to believe in, but I can understand from going to a nonbeliever to a believer. As a child, I was very ill for a couple of months. I may have been broken down by abuse, but I never stopped believing in God. Every night when I was in the hospital for a couple of months, I never forgot to get down on my knees and pray.

Sometimes when you think your child is safe in certain places, that may not be the case. When I was in the hospital due to neglect and abuse by the hand of some family members and sometimes by the hands of a babysitter, something has happened in the hospital, something I have witnessed happen to other children. Children see what they should not see, or any child should have to endure. Sometimes, when in the hospital for a mental breakdown, that's what happened to me as a child. I just could not take the abuse any longer My mind was strained. I was such a pretty child and smart too.

I knew something was happening to me, but I did not know what; but before I went through all what I have been going through, it was odd. I prayed to God to help me. I put on my prettiest dress and a red rose and laid down in my bed. I said something like "Dear Lord, something's going on with me. I don't know what. I present myself to you with my prettiest dress. Please be with me, Lord." My mother was in denial that something was wrong with me I'm not myself. When my family came over, I was crying. I know I freaked my brothers out, but still, a neighbor had to tell my mother to get me help. My mother still was in denial, then two friends tried to tell her. Finally, she realized I was in really bad shape. I went from a junior's misses five, six to a child's size fourteen clothing. I could no longer talk just sounds but not words like a person who never learned how to speak. I was going backwards with the quickness. My mother told me that she thought that I was going to die. God saved me. I was not on any medication. My father wanted it to be a secret; besides, he felt it would ruin my life and people to prejudge me, so I kept it a secret. Some of my family members treated me nice, but at the same time, it made me feel like I would always be the crazy cousin. I was just broken down for a child and did not know where to turn to. When I got on my feet for a long time, I did not like to take pills of any kind. It seems like that part of my childhood when I made recovery that it did not even happen to me, and that it had happen to someone else. I treat people the way I want to be treated. When people try to put me down and say I think am something, if they only knew this is who I am, but they don't know that I was a caring little girl for a couple of months who knew no one but God and just hanging by her faith. I had a great aunt who passed away. She was tough, but I knew she was praying for me. She was the opposite of Great-Great Rosie when it came down to religion. Great-Great Auntie Rosie spoiled me and taught me how to respect myself. Great Auntie Gwen taught me the true value of religion and was very very strict when it came to mannerism. In New York, I could dance, say the word doggone it. I could not dance around Great Auntie Gwen. One of the cousins said before Great Auntie Gwen passed away, she said I was truly going to make something out of myself, but she never told me. These were the greatest women I knew, Great-Great Auntie Rosie from New York and Great Auntie Gwen from California. They were both in the business for care of their families. One aunt lived in New York and one lived in California; for that, I am grateful to have someone so dear in each state I lived in. There are so many things that say "statistics shows" or the saying "apples do not fall far from the tree."

A person does not have to be a negative statistic. If apples do not fall far from the tree, it does not mean the apple has to be rotten. I know whatever negative cycle that was swirling around me, I wanted not to be better than anyone but not to go down that same road. It's funny when you are trying in life that people around you feel that they are not where they needed to be wanted to compete with. If they are giving you such a hassle, maybe you need to fall back. They are people who are so unhappy with their lives they will try to mess up yours or try to do harm to you mentally or even physically. I know loneliness is a lonely word, but sometimes, it's good to be alone. Being alone is not at all a bad idea. Sometimes, I get lonely. I remember several years ago, there was a person singing a song so beautifully. One of my favorite songs and several people in the church started to cry including myself. I thought about the bridge over troubled waters that I was going through. As the song played, and it was the same song I requested while in Bible study. I cried buckets, and I thought of my family. When I was able to help them, they were always around and how I missed them. Let's talk about jobs. When you are looking for a job and it's a job that you are interested in but do not fit, some of the educational qualifications apply anyway. When they say experience is the best teacher, they are telling the truth. A relative of mine was a counselor and did not even have a college degree. People were getting jealous of him at work, and these were the people who have master's degree and bachelor's degree. I always thought that I should have been doing better in life than I was.

There would always be a feeling in my soul when I needed to do something for the better. There would be this feeling that there was some type of hidden gift that I had inside of me that I did not know I had. Like the great Reverend Jessie Jackson would say; it went something like this: "I am somebody, I am somebody, you are somebody, you are somebody." This week has been a very interesting week. Let's rewind. I got on the prayer phone line at 6:00 a.m. That's really not my time of the day unless I was studying or needed to be somewhere within that hour. The prayer line was so enlightening. I applied for a job within the company, and I got contacted to come in for an interview for a great position. Someone who I have not heard from in a while, I heard from him today. I was so excited. I heard back from the water department that they want me to pay at least $1,100 before they turn back on my water. That was the fee that they said why they did not turn my water back on, but they were sending me a bill every month. I told them I don't care about the fee. I did not know nothing about that. As far as I knew, the department turned it on and was billing me because I was getting the bills. A lesson for me and hopefully for you all too. Your utilities make sure you do not fall so far behind even in your rent. If you pay rent, do not get so far behind that you are sitting in front of the people or person in charge of where you live debating what happened, what you owed and the how, when and where factor. The water department is going to do a payment plan for me, praise the Lord. God is always in the midst of things even when it looks like a hopeless case. I went to visit a church, and the pastor was telling a story about footprints in the sand. The pastor went on to speak there was only one set of footprints in the sand. There were one set of footprints because God was carrying the person. Staying focus can be hard for me. Maybe I get so distracted with the chain of events. There is a lot of motivational people today. A lot of times, a person may make things seem so easy, but little steps at a time, and before one knows it, the goal is reached, or bill is paid. Getting a recorder to tape what you want to do if writing a book helps a lot. When I get an idea and not feeling like grabbing the laptop or writing it down, a recorder is a good device to have. What I learned in life when things are not turning out like you may want it, do not be too hard on yourself. Try to put a little more effort, even if you think you have done what you can. This week, I am going to challenged myself, better yet for the rest of the month, I will add to my book. So, once I make my entries in the book on a regular basis, before I know it, it will be completed. This is one of my philosophies I have in life; no matter when it will be finished as long as the goal or whatever you are working on will be completed. Of course, meeting deadlines are very important. A lot of things are done according to a time frame. Meeting deadlines can be very good in life. Set a time you want a goal to be completed or when you think is the best time to get your goal or deadline completed. I have found in life that some people are very competitive and want to compete with you, and you may not want to be competitive. I learned to be competitive with myself. Each day that God allows me to wake up, I try to do better than I did the day before. This very statement I was told got me to start to move up the corporate. I have learned over the years no matter how hard life may be or how many times people want to put you down, still love yourself. Some people are so quick to judge without even asking questions, but once they find out the truth, some tend to act more compassionately, and some still do not care. I say to myself how quickly can one turn from snarling up at you to giving you a pity hug. I don't understand. A true friend can be just like family. So the times you have cut a person or certain people loose, because the relationship is doing more harm to you than help. I am no doctor, I've been through so much, but I have seen worst.

Recently, there have been a lot of rain. So much rain that less than five minutes from where I live, they needed those rubber raftlike boats to go back and forth. So many homes were flooded mainly in basements. My heart went out to the people whose cars were almost submerged in water. This area is where I may often have shopped. I even brought my last car from the area. There is a lot of flood and backups in the streets and pipelines here. I do not have a basement, have a serious backup off and on. I got a pipe repaired leading from my home to the street, and then eventually, I had to get a small tree pulled and a pipe replaced. I had another backup a couple of years later, so I have definitely learned to get my pipeline leading from the house to the streets cleaned or checked at least once a year, just like I would get my furnace once a year. Sometimes, a tool served a purpose you never know when it would be great for something else. I have decided to see if I can get another house. I will keep the one I am in. Owning a property is a great thing to have. I struggled so hard to get my home. If I rent it out, I hope I can rent it out to a family that will appreciate it just as much as I do. When I first pulled up to the house, I said to myself this is the home I want for my three children and myself. Each of them was blessed to have their own bedroom. I would like to buy another home. I remember my goal was to own three homes, but my hardships in life cause me to stray from my dreams. I had so many dreams in life. For example, I wanted to become a business owner. Things have changed a lot. Now a business is more than a stationary productive building. The key these days is creativity. Be daring, so I decided to see if I can buy another home. The only thing the realtor can say is the deal went through or the deal not go through. I would like to relocate to another state. Sometimes, change is good. I admire anyone who can pick up and move to another city. I know it will take some adjusting and soul searching. Before I relocate, I am going to visit the city a couple of times to make sure it is truly the place for me. Even though my children are adults, I would love for us all to relocate to the same city. I know someone, and their family brought some land out of state, and the whole several family members lived on the same street, how cool is that, especially when you all can get along. If I attempt to get the car, somewhere down the line, I am blessed with a couple of times of having a great car. Next step is to work on getting another home. Maybe God was saving my dreams on a shelf until I came back from my journey of darkness. God never left me. Just like a parent watching their child from afar. A child may think he is walking alone when not far away, his parent is watching. I know dreams were swept away from my mind, but God kept them, but never in a million years I thought I would be writing a book. If you have to file taxes, it's so much cheaper to file them yourself. For years, I went in to agencies and file my taxes. At first, I used to file them myself. The only reason I started to go and pay a couple hundred dollars for a fast refund, another reason I wanted to see if there were any more credits I can get. There are a lot of places these days where you can go and get your taxes done free of charge. You can do so much with your income tax check, but remember you cannot buy the world with it. I hear so much about the word focus. So much encouragement from the movers and shakers of the world. This past week, I was having trouble sleeping; to me, that is a rough situation, especially when you have to get up the next morning. I am glad that the Lord woke me up and got me on my way. I realize it's a struggle, but God brought me through. I hope my readers learned something from my book. Sometimes, when you are the oldest child such as myself, you don't have a lot of role models to choose from. You are expected to be the role model. Even though being the oldest of my siblings had its challenges, I would not trade it away for anything. I treat people the way I want to be treated. Unfortunately, sometimes, it's hard to work with people when you do not feel the same. My favorite saying is "killing them with kindness" is true. You do not have to beg anyone to be your friend. I could never understand why a person did not like me especially as a child. After all, I never cause confusion in school. I wasn't a bully. My mom gave me the harsh reality. As a child, she told me everyone will not like me. I'll never forget Great-Great Aunt Rosie brought me some beautiful boots. They were called go-go boots. They were a little above the ankle and were black patent leather that zip up the back. I was about in the second grade, and this other little girl said to me, "You think you are something because you have on some go-go boots?" I remember as a child I never felt that I thought I was something. I went home and told Great Great Auntie Rosie what happened that day in school. The very next day, that same little girl had on the exact pair of go-go boots I had on. I was not upset, but I did tell Auntie Rosie about the little girl the next day having on the same boots that I had on. Auntie Rosie sent my older cousin and me shopping to get me a pair of beautiful white go-go boots that zip on the side more like a cowboy-style boot. Several times through out of my adult life, people tell me that I think I am something. Once again, I am disappointed because that is not the case. I am saying this to tell that sometimes people are jealous, or they wish they had your style and personality. I was raised to be humble. Everyone deserves to be happy and to express themselves. I said that some adults and children behave in the same manner. People would tell me that my children were so well behaved in public. I would tell them thank you, and you do not know how it gets when the curtain goes down. I would joke and say it's all a performance you should be around once the curtain comes down. One of my college degrees is Bachelor of Arts. I would tell my children when we go out into the world, you all are doing a performance like you are on stage.

CHAPTER

9

I FEEL LIKE I HAVE GONE through the trial of fire. I have always looked for the light in the end of the tunnel. I always wonder why was it so difficult for me. I wanted different and better life for my children. I wanted them to catch their dreams faster than I could ever imagine myself being in life. Trial by fire in Bible reading is found in James 1:12; this is a powerful verse: at one of my prison visits to see my son Joey, he read this to me through a glass window over the telephone, and there are so many people that are going through trial by fire. James 1:12, "Blessed is the one who preserves under the trial because, having stood the test, that person will receive the crown of life." It seems like God is handing me back my dreams and thoughts that were so far and in the back of my mind, they were almost gone. People need to accept you for who you are and what positive path you have in life. If they do not want to respect you for what you are trying to do in life, be careful. Sometimes, those same people will try to take advantage of you or even act like they are going to help you, and they get information from you. They do not help you at all the same information you have given them. They use it for something else. You have to live your life to the fullest, be happy, because true happiness is not easy to find for everyone, myself included. I have always had in my thoughts, in my mind and in my dreams to relocate. I know if I was not brought here as a child, I would still be in New York. I love New York. I am an adult, and I love being one.

I enjoy being an adult because I have the opportunity to change my life. My biggest mistake is allowing people to be a part of my life who only made me feel bad, and once I realize that they only created confusion and heartaches. I still struggled to let them go due to the love I gave them, and they did not know how to accept it. I still have to learn and have to deal with everyone I have accepted for whatever reason they do not want to accept me. Whatever the case may be, just move on and follow the path you were supposed to follow.

I know I have had these moments in life where there is a void. I just did not know what I was supposed to be doing, but I knew it was something. The void was very powerful; it was like an itch that would not rest until I scratched it. I love music back in the day. I would dance, and my moves would just flow with the music. I have read that if you listen to music fifteen minutes before you go to sleep, it will help. A couple of weeks ago, I could not sleep, but I had to get up; business as usual. I was so wired up with all the negative things that I was dealing with that it became overwhelming. Some people are quick to judge they will stare you in the face and say what all you are not doing, but never asking what can they do to assist in making it better. I have no time to belittle anyone. Always try to better yourself. Just when you think there is no room for improvement, be your own critic and create another goal for yourself. You know truly about some folk with you in thick and thin, just stop helping them financially. Some folks think that you may be too old to finish your goals or even start new ones. There is a shop owner that owns a chain of stores, and every time I go in his original store, he is at the same cash register and ringing out groceries. This man is very close to being one hundred years of age. He's very generous in the community. This owner of this store is a very ambitious person. I used to be afraid of change. I was seventeen years old when I graduated from high school, and I was afraid of success. I read in a book that basically being afraid of success is a normal way to feel. My question is perhaps I was never around people who was successful themselves, everything was on a basis of life survival.

Recently, I thought to myself some not-so-good thoughts. I decided to write this in my book, and hopefully, whoever is struggling with life like I have been so many times can say yes, the struggle is real, but as God is my witness and my provider, I will fight to survive and also work on my goals at the same time. Recently, I had thoughts in my head; it was very tough and harsh reality is what I had on myself. I thought, Sophie, everything you were going to do as an adult at this point in your life is not all done, except getting a degree from institution of higher learning. I worked long hours and sometimes two jobs to provide for my family.

What I learned is if I worked two jobs to survive, take some time to work on my goals and a plan. I spend my money much better when I write down. Who I am going to pay at what time and how much and when. It's better to have a grocery list when you go grocery shopping. I remember when my children were smaller, I would put the grocery list and stick it on the refrigerator and let the children know to add what they want on it. No matter how busy I was, I made sure I took the time out with my children. I did not allow them to go house to house to trick or treat because I heard too many horrible stories about candy being tainted with harmful things. I was really afraid to allow my children to spend the night over people's houses for a long time; because of the abuse I had endured in the past. Because the abuse had taken such a toll on me when I was a child in my relatives' homes. I was afraid to take my children to them. I do not regret it either because of the remarks they make to me now when I see them and the remarks that they made behind my back that they don't know I knew about. Auntie Rosie told me everything didn't have to be told. I struggled with this book because I never had this on my agenda of goals. Some say it's okay to tell all, and some say it's not. I am just letting the world know that you'll be surprise who struggles in life, who comes home to be lonely, whose children are in trouble. The world is so cold these days, even one's own family truly do not care what's going on in their other family member's life if it is not benefitting them or because you chose a different path. Life is a journey; if you get knocked down, get back up. A lesson for life too; when I watched a basketball game, a person accidently falls on the floor. If they can get up and usually they can, they do. In life, you can take a lesson from basketball players, when you get down, get up with the quickness and continue on with your goals, and at the end, basketball players a goal, which is just like mine, it's good to win or be a winner. These days, a lot in the world is so dangerous. Sometimes to me, it seems like the world is spinning back in time. I pray that it gets better, for the world and for the struggles of families out there. I thought I would always be living in my home that I fought too hard to get and God in front of me fighting my battles. When I think I am alone, I am not because God is with me. I believe in God because of my faith and what he's done for me. I hope I have done something to make a difference in someone's life. I do not need a metal or plaque. I just hope when I help someone, I really made a difference. My thought process is that if you help someone and they keep getting themselves in the same old rut and come back to again, are you really helping? Do they really understand that it's to assist you getting back on track and not staying off track and coming back to you with the same old story? "Sometimes, life is hard for no reason at all," and sometimes, we make so many mistakes that we made life hard for ourselves. I know I am not perfect, and I had made a lot of mistakes. I have learned not to beat myself up about it and not allow those who try to mentally beat me up, nor let their words stick to my soul, because it will, like at a darkness on one's soul, don't give them the satisfaction of thinking that you allow them to beat you down mentally. I do my best to stay prayed up and pack my bags for my next journey in life. When I used to get in trouble with my parents as a child, one of my little brothers used to tease me and say, "How does it feel like ice cream?" That saying can have some positive meanings. I had a really productive day or feeling in some type of really positive way. I think I could really get some good ice cream; it makes me feel better. Like during this segment, I made me an ice-cream float. Sometimes, you have to think outside the box.

My daughter used to laugh every time I would pull up to a drive through fast food and ask for a float. I just had a float. My favorite one would be vanilla ice cream with Pepsi or Coca-Cola. Most of the fast food restaurants would say no. Every time we went to a drive-thru, I would ask the same thing. Could I have a float? One day, I went to a drive- thru My daughter and I asked for a float even though the restaurant did not sell them. The customer service representative sold me a float. My daughter and I were laughing so hard. I'm saying about the float to say that sometimes, we have to step out of our comfort zone or outside the box. Sometimes, we have the tools right in front of us to start, something new without even realizing the possibilities until we try and in a lot of cases succeed. When you are on a journey to something, just because someone tells you they do not have what you want does not mean that you have to give up and stop trying. Thinking outside the box is good. It also comes around when you least expect it, and it feels just like cool and a refreshing ice-cream taste. Right now, I am really going through trials, but when I heard what someone else is going through, I say to myself, "Wow, there is always someone whose situation is worst."

As I was driving, I have $17 in my pocket and to my name, but I was very grateful for the $17. I can go get me something to eat. While I was driving, I was also thinking of my unfinished goals. I struggled to get them started, and I should have been finished. I am struggling to get them finished. A lesson I have learned when putting more effort or too much in one area of life, you do not have enough willpower to go forth in areas that can be really beneficial to your struggle. I listen and watch and hear about people reaching their goals, and some even encourage others. Then there are some folks who are not willing to help anyone, and they only hang around the well-to-do folks. There are also folks who, no matter how much you try to help them as long as you help them, will never be able to stand on their two feet. When you can no longer help them because you just do not have it, then they do not call you, or if they are in the neighborhood, they will not even stop by to see you. Then there are some folks who, since you are unable to help them anymore, want to portray you to others as a bad person. I have learned the hard way as a child, but sometimes, my personality cannot be understood. When you are kind to someone, why do they have a hard time accepting the fact that you are kind, and they return meanness and conflict back to you? Jealousy is a mean hard word. I had a boss who said she was jealous of me. Was she joking, or did she admire my struggles and how I took it on? I told her not to be jealous of me. You have everything, and plus, some than I do have, including finances. She has always been better off financially than me. Sometimes, when you are struggling, maybe your struggles are struggles that someone else will gladly take and run away with it. What may be a struggle to you, there is something in that struggle that is special that someone else wish they had. Maybe someone may have wanted to accomplish a goal at some point in their lives, and even in the midst of your struggles, you have accomplished it. I see more and more where people are coming out and saying they do not believe in God the Heavenly Father, the Creator of the universe. There are people who went to churches where they believed in God and faith was practiced, and for some reason, they lost faith. What could have happened to them or someone else they knew that changed their hearts, mind and soul in another direction when it comes to God and belief. They may be successful financially, and have a great life, but God and faith they are not believing. I accept people for who they are; after all, it's been in my soul since I was a child. Why if I accept you as you are, can't you accept me? Am I in position to judge or try to always persuade to have someone be like me? We all have been created to make choices in life; we also have been created to change our minds. I was reading a statement someone has written about how certain religion does not go visit people who are in jail. Not everyone in jail is guilty.

The late great Dr. Martin Luther King Jr. was in jail, and more than once fighting for something that people should not have to fight for since President Lincoln changed the course of time. A lot of people went to jail with Dr. Martin Luther King. There are a host of other people who have been in jail and maybe innocent. The late great Harriet Tubman was freeing slaves; certain parts of the country did not have slaves. If she was caught, she would have been hung or shot. In some parts of the country, slavery was a crime and other parts in history it was not. Although slavery should have never been in the first place. Even to this day, there have been some people in jail who, after being incarcerated for years, have been deemed innocent.

Basically, One Pastor said you should forgive, but you don't have to forget. What was basically said even though you forgive? It doesn't mean that the relationship has to continue the way it was? My life was tough too. I wrote this book because there are so many people in the world who are struggling to have the will to survive. I wrote this book because there are people who are judging someone based on the outside, without knowing what was really going on. You cannot judge a book by its cover. Making plans when you are young, it sometimes does not happen the way you plan it. I just do not believe it. I went to college based on my dreams I had when I was a teen. When I was a child, I always wanted to have some type of glamorous lifestyle. In life, some people always want you to live the way they think you should live it. Happiness does not come easy for everyone. It's good to be happy. Happiness starts within yourself. It seems like it takes much more energy and makes one feel bad to be angry or sad. Sometimes, everyone does not like to see you happy; you just have to keep your head up and keep moving. It seems to me that when I think about no matter how successful or others think I am, I think I can always use room for improvement.

I think I need room for improvement because I never want to be broke. I want not to have to wear the same clothes every week. Once I heard someone say that you should not be seen with the same outfit on no longer than two weeks at a time. When you are not making the money that you know you should be making can cut your wardrobe back. You can do a lot of mix and match. Do not feel bad that you do not have all the beautiful clothes; sometimes, clothing has to be put on credit, and then you have to pay the bill. It comes in handy when you work in a department store, and you have to make your quota for the day, and you get the sale, and guess what? A credit card is used. Do not feel bad because if it was not for credit, a lot of people would not be able to get the things they have. Credit can be a good thing, but the bill if not paid in full has interest. A lot of time we just cannot use cash to buy everything. There's nothing wrong with credit because you can save your money and put it toward something else like a bill. To fall behind on credit is not good. You may really need to use that card, and because of late payments, you will not be able to use the card. During my freshman year, this speaker came to our all-girl dormitory and told us we should spend what we have. One friend I had suggested to me to take out a very large loan. Is society okay with living in debt? Are the people who made these comments so well off that they can give this information to others, not knowing what their financial situation at that current time? There is nothing wrong with going to the goodwill to buy clothes. I found a couple of nice winter coats that I brought at the goodwill, one was for $10, and the other one was for $12. I'm sure these coats cost a lot more than $10 and $12 originally. I used to work in a department store, and we had to ticket and mark down the items. The department store was a high-end store. The employees would every so often get 65 percent off from the red tag plus their regular employee discount. To me, that was the best time to shop. I find that making out a budget just like you do a grocery list helps a lot too. If a person is not happy with their present situation and if it is possible to change it by all means do so. I always tell myself if I am not happy with my present situation, usually most of the time I have the power to change it. It's a matter of moving forward with your life. Someone told me while I was standing at a bus stop that I look like I should be riding in a Cadillac. Someone once told me I give good advice, so I should be following the same advice myself. I was truly speaking from experience, and I did not wish some of the struggles that I went through. If I could have helped someone to not go through what I've been through or to help them to avoid it, I would. Everyone could use a word of encouragement, a hug, and smile once in a while. Patience is a good thing to have. You never know what a person is going through. You think your story is the worse because you have endured it, but there is someone whom their story is worst. It's funny when people think they know you and really do not. The big word that was told to me is confidence and owning something.

When you work hard and someone tells you that you do not have enough confidence, it can sometimes make you feel broken or defeated, but do not give up. I googled the word confidence on my iPhone. Now it's different from being arrogant or too much pride. The word confidence in Google was written as Confidence/|Psychology Today. - Confidence can be described as a belief in one's ability to succeed. Striking a healthy balance can be challenging. Too much of it and you can come off as cocky and stumble into unforeseen obstacles, but having too little can prevent you from taking risks and seizing opportunities." Sometimes, you may have to step up your confidence if people are trying to on a regular basis put you down. Why do some people try to put other people down? Is it to knock them down mentally in life, or is it to attempt to build up their own ego? The term negative people is a difficult term to me because it appears that people are being labeled in a box into one category. There are so many ways these days you can change how you look. People tell me I look like the great and beautiful actress Pam Grier. One day, I was in an expensive department store, and someone told me I looked like the late great singer actress Lena Horne. I find it all complimenting. I always wanted to either be in the glamour of life even as a child. There is also another side of me that would like to help people. Sometimes, when you help people, they take your kindness for weakness. Some folks when you cannot help them any-more or stop helping them, they stop coming around, will not call you unless they want something, or even have the nerve to point out negative things about you, but not the good. Whether they are fam-ily or supposed to be friends, you may have to change your circle of who you hang around. I had to learn the hard way. I have a couple of sayings. At least I never heard anyone used these sayings before. "If you don't want anything told, don't tell it," and "Everyone business not everyone's business." I have a saying about my goals. They are called Sophie's goals: ABCMG, which means always be closing my goals. I push myself so hard because I know I should be doing better. I know there are so many negative things going on in my life that some days, I just do not have the strength to make it better. Then I get the strength to make the move on. I can go to work every day and give 110 percent, but I am so broken inside that I cannot give 110 percent for myself. Wow, after this last sentence, I have rebooted myself and my energy. I fast during the lent season to give up something for the period that I really enjoy. You do not always have to fast by not eating. Everyone cannot go without food. If I do not eat by a certain time of the day, I get an upset stomach and a terrible headache, and I will vomit. Once I start to feel ill from not eating in a timely manner, once I do eat, it's too late. I am already ill. No matter what you got going on and what needs to be done, always get your rest, sleep and eat right. I feel much better when I get some rest. I am more of a night owl, but I feel much better when I get a good night's sleep. When I wanted to strengthen my vocabulary every day, I would pick a word out of the dictionary and look up the meaning. I found it very useful, and it broadened my vocabulary to pick a word from the dictionary. I hear this saying love yourself because if you do not, who will? Whenever you think you cannot, you probably could, you just needed to work a little harder. Education is so important. College is a big deal, but nowadays, just one high school diploma or GED (General Education Development) is a big struggle. My hats go off to the students these days who can get out of high school. There are a lot of people who are being very creative in starting their own business (entrepreneurs). Maybe the goals I had as a child were not the goals that God had for me. Sometimes, life gets tough, but to keep going, sometimes, your own family may laugh at you and try to make you look like a bad person, but you got to keep going. I believe in setting an example. Always say set an example and not be made an example of. If things do not work out the way you want it, do not give up, perhaps you may have to go to another route.

Once a person gets discouraged, it's hard trying to get out of that funk. Every day that we wake up could be an opportunity to complete or start working on our goals. When I mentor, I ask what do a person want to do five years from now. I ask some people in their thirties, and they do not know. If I ask them more than once over a period of time, they get a little perturbed. Just because a person is in a low-income status does not mean that one has to stay that way. Sometimes, people have the tendency having a hard time adjusting to change, whether it be witnessing someone else change or accepting their own change.

When I was starting college, I was afraid of the big step I was taking. I was the first in my family to receive a college degree. Sometimes, you can still be kind to the people who you were kind to before you went to college, but sometimes, they just treat you like you no longer fit in. You think back you may not have fitted in a group in the first place. I always wanted folks to accept me, but like someone once told me years ago, if they do not, that is their problem. Staying healthy is such a good thing. Now it is mandatory that people have medical insurance, if not there is a hefty fine. If we have medical, we should use it. I found a dental office that's open seven days a week until 9:00 p.m. I have been scheduling something once a month to go to the doctor. You have to love yourself and part of loving yourself is taking care of yourself. You are no good to anyone else if you become ill. I never used my sick leave for two years because I was saving my sick time in case I needed it for one of my three children who will get sick. I had gotten so ill, and I was being diagnosed with the wrong illness. I was still going to work, I felt like a baby learning to walk.

I was so concerned with the unknown of just exactly what was going on with me. I would sleep with my Bible under my pillow for comfort. I went to another hospital, and I was diagnosed with asthma after a year of going through. I remember listening to the *Tom Joyner Morning Show* over the radio because it just brought comfort to my soul, and it helped me deal with whatever I was going through as I was driving across the freeway struggling with my unknown illness, taking my children to the day care and then heading to work. I said that one day, I would write Mr. Joyner and let him know that I found comfort listening to his show while I was driving on the road when I was ill. Maybe he will read my book, and this is like my appreciating how his show touches a lot of lives. People talk about tomorrow is not promised to no one but can change so suddenly that it is mind-boggling.

I never forgot the early part of the day I was running errands and even did a little dancing at the house. I called my brother and said I am having an allergic reaction. The next thing I knew, I had gone into anaphylactic shock. I remember someone at church got upset with me because the children were in the Christmas program and I was just in no shape to bring them, nor did they volunteer to come get my children. It took a whole year to fix the problem with my illness. Sometimes, people can be on a mission not realizing that they are being insensitive along the way. My son says that when we are in a jam, I would say it's all good, or it's going to be alright.

I said and still do use those terms that "it's all good and its going be alright." My faith is so strong, and my beliefs in the heavenly Father's powers I truly believe that" with man, it may be impossible, but with God, it is possible." In the Bible from Mark 10:27, Jesus looked at them and said, "With man, this is impossible, but not with God: all things are possible with God."

CHAPTER

10

I T'S REALLY SOMETHING THAT SOMETIMES, people will make fun of your failures and remind you of your failed success, but it's all good because the success that I wanted was not the type of success was written for me. Jobs are so competitive these days, some states have fire at will and other states do not.

I know people who live in states that do not have the fire-at-will law, and I know people who do live in the fire-at-will states. I do not know what's the answer, but it seems to me that the people who I know hold their jobs a lot longer is in the do not fire-at-will states. It is always good to send a thank-you note. Since this is the computer age, it is acceptable to send a thank-you e-mail. To look different, follow up the thank you e-mail or a letter saying the exact same thing that was on the e-mail sent. You must check over your resumes even if they are professionally done. Once I checked over someone's resume, that was done professionally. This person had just graduated from college, and the most important thing that was missing was that a college degree was earned. A short thank-you note is in order; we have to stand out in the hiring process. There are some companies that will tell you that do not call them, make sure you understand the hiring process and not call. It's so much easier when a company do not have stipulation on the following up. I remember one company I worked for hired me about five to six months after the interview for a job. In the meantime, I made sure that I was positive with just keeping my name on the hiring table. All the holidays I made sure I sent the person that interviewed me a card. Eventually, I was hired and was there for a very long time. What I have learned through my journey I have become successful not by a title or by how much money I make or even how nice I am to others. Success means to the trials and tribulations that I or anyone may endure and how it was handled. It's good to follow your dreams, and if you could not do them until later in life, it's not too late. In these days and times, try not to worry so much, live a little. Once a month if you are on a budget, do something fun. Sometimes, job hopping is not the best thing to do all the time. If you got your position working like a well-oiled machine, and you applied for a position, don't get it. Just get another position maybe within the company where you can be utilized better. When we put on our resumes and thank-you cards that we know, we can make the company better or be a great asset to the company when you are hired; that is exactly what the company expects. I have learned in life that money does pay the bills, but some jobs are really tough, and then you have to wonder why did I just stay at the position I was at? I got it under control. How you look on your resume is what your employer expected you to look like while you're doing your job. It's just best to tell the truth when you're creating your resume because the truth will come out and you'll be able to do what you can do. I find it very rewarding to take some time off to myself in about a couple of days. Those days off work; it's always good to do something to relax yourself and have fun. Going one tank trips can be fun. There used to be this show on television that showed various interesting places that one can visit and come back home all in the same day. There were great people in my life.

My late Uncle Leon and I used to love to go to the store with him when I was a little girl. We used to have really good conversations. Even though he passed away too soon, it seemed to me that he enjoyed life, and life had not cheated him none because he lived life to the fullest. Great-Great Auntie Rosie was in her seventies, and she was gone too soon also. Life had not cheated her none either because she moved from various states, and every state she lived in she was always the glue that held the family together. Life is only what we make it. Some may have to work harder than others. To maintain what you have, it has to be taken care of even if someone is taking care of it for you. The reason I'm writing this book is because sometimes, even your people can misjudge you or being mean to you because you chose a direction. You still want to hang out with people you used to hang out with, but they may say something to you or treat you differently because you and them choose a different path of life. I wrote this book because it is very discerning for people to greet me with a frown instead of a hug. I wrote this book because people should really get to know someone instead of believing what other people say. Everyone should treat themselves like queens and kings. We are so important; the human race is the most beautiful creation. We all look different; we come from various race and ethnicity, but at the end of the day, we are all humans. I do my very best to be humble. It is so funny when you try to mind your own business and some adults will try to pick with you or try to put you down. There is no educational or financial status that a person is in they just pick with you for no reason at all, are they bullies? Who knows. I was taught when people talk about you negatively, there must be something about you they like.

Education is so important. When it comes down to education, it is so important to understand what is going on in life. It is better to have education than not to have education at all. It is better to have education and money, than just to have education and no money at all. There is nothing worse than to hear about some educated person taking advantage of a person that has money but no education. Getting your high school diploma or GED is so important because that is the beginning to your road to success. To me, having this education have helped me to handle things in a different manner, then I would have handled it if I did not. All those classes that I had to take, even those that I thought would not help me in life did. I talked about my childhood because I believed that my past has something to do with my present, and my present will have something to do with my future. Being abuse as a child has taught me that you cannot put nothing pass anyone. I once read in a book that when someone do not treat you right, they will not treat your children right. I never understood why people mistreat children. When I got one of my college degrees I was just working in a department store, but I kept feeling this void in my life. I prayed to God about the void in my life. My prayers were answered I became very involved in church activities. I taught Sunday school for a long time. I volunteered in missionary groups, the choir and other volunteer activities. When I was a child, I was a Brownie with the girl scouts. When I was in the sixth grade even though I was abused, I got good grades in school and enjoyed singing in the choir. The choir would just go from school to school. With all my bouts in life, I graduated from high school at the age of seventeen years; I never failed a grade or was held back. My family was poor enough so I could get a summer job. The summer job that I got right out of high school was to go back to the very high school that I went to teach business math, which I have never taken I taken algebra. This goes to show you that you do not have to have experience in something, just the willing to try and the passion to help others and yourself. I am very blessed because somehow, I had the willpower to push on. Stay humble all the way. I learned early that life is not always a bowl of cherries, sometimes you get the pits of the cherries. I never liked competition. I always thought if we are on the same team, why not be a team. The person that I am competing with is myself. I challenge myself to do better. When I had my three children, as an unwed mother, I taught them the best I could. The only thing I just prayed for God is to watch over my children. Even though I am almost done with this book, Joey is still in jail. I cannot afford the bail to get him out of jail, even after putting up our house for the bail. Once in the judicial system, it is very hard to get out. I am not mad at God, I do not blame God for what has happened. Sometimes, I say this is a nightmare with what's going on with my son that I have not woken up from what is happening to my family? My other children have graduated from college, and have moved out of the home. My children are always welcome back to my home. I now can do some transformation like an office and a movie room. I do not have a degree in social services or psychology by not an expert of anything. I just wanted to share my story and of my life. I treat people the way I want to be treated. In my opinion, the world would be a much better place if there was more love and kindness in it.

I guess you can call me a night owl. I always stay up late. It's late now. I just want to continue to finish my book. I am almost done. As I complete this book, it's funny how most people see me as successful. I am really struggling in life. My dreams have changed a lot over the years from wanting to own a couple of boutiques to just trying to survive in life. When you are young, please be careful who you choose as friends and do not hang around folks that do not want you around them, hoping that they may change their minds. Speaking from experience, they will turn on you for any kind of reason. As I wrap up this book, I never intended to become a writer. As a matter of fact in college, I had to take eleven English classes because my writing was not at its best. I brought books about writing, and I found out that it helped a lot. I loved to read true stories about famous businesspeople and how they got started. A lot of them struggled and have taken a great risk. To me, it's good to hear how successful people started because, in my opinion, people go by what they see and not knowing what kind of a risk or gamble the person has taken to be successful. So much has happened since I am finishing up this book.

My daughters are both college graduates and are in their first apartments. Joey's trial is coming up in a couple of months. I pray that he would be found not guilty and can come home. I have been thinking about maybe renting my home out to a family. I say this because this house has been such a blessing to my family, and I do not want to sell it, but I would like to relocate to another state. Time flies so fast before I knew it, my children are grown-ups. So far, I have not met a new love of my life, but one day, I hope I do. I never understood why I have no one yet, but hopefully, I will meet the man of my dreams.

One thing I have done by being single is to work long hours especially when it needs to be done. I started working on my book and finishing it. I can relocate to another state without debating with anyone. Of course, I would have to come back to visit and check on my house that I fought long and hard to get. I tell everyone I am no doctor, but I do know this from my experience that life is what you make it.

If you have a chance to catch up life, do it. You are never too old. In early part of my story, I spoke about the store manager in the nineties still keeping his shop. He owned a chain of stores. I believe he did not have to ring at the cash register. He checked out sales because he wanted too, and he loved what he is doing. Do what you love to do in life. I know finances at times can be a great factor on what one wants to do in life. Even though there are jobs in life that I may not like, I work the job and do it to the best of my ability. I smiled, I was very polite to everyone, went to work all while I was looking for another job. I always used one of my jobs a life lesson now. I have two jobs that I can use as a life lesson. I have always been a humble person, and one job I had one summer, I was fourteen years old when I chopped weeds for the summer. In my adult life, the most challenging job I had was after my full-time job. I washed cars for a rental car franchise, and the do it all year long in snow weather. They also did a count on how many cars you cleaned and washed. When I was at home and had to wash my car, I learned to time myself that it should only take me fifteen minutes (laugh out loud). The best job that I had was after graduating from high school. I was the assistant business math teacher for the summer. I graded papers and figured out grades and tutored the children. When I was offered the job, I did not know that I would be teaching in the same high school that I graduated from. Some of the children should have graduated in the same class that I graduated in but did not, so they were going to summer school so that they could graduate soon.

In high school, it was so important to make sure you have the credits you need to graduate. It's good to keep in touch with your guidance counselor so you can see what needs to be taken to graduate and what does not need to be taken. You have to make sure that all your books are turned back in the school. I made one mistake of giving my science book to a student who was waiting for the teacher because I went there, and the teacher was not there yet. However, I did do something smart. I went back to the teacher and asked if the student gave him my book, and guess what? He said no, he had not received it. I asked him the cost of the book, and I paid for it. If a student owed money when they call your name to get your cap and gown, you either got the cap and gown, or you were given a note on what was owed. I was very glad to get my cap and gown. Despite all the hardships and abuses causing me to collapse as a child mentally, I never failed a grade and graduated on time. I wrote this book because I always dreamt and still do that there is light and rainbow waiting at the end of the tunnel. My friends would tell me I do not know how you do what you do. They were referring to how I've gotten around not depending on anyone despite what anyone thought. Sometimes, my friend would say to me jokingly that I just don't give a damn. They would joke about my demeanor, and I did not show fear or hesitation. I never gave up trying to better my life. I remained calm.

What had given me strength was and still is my belief and faith in God. I do not know what I would have done without him. I get inspired just driving down the street and seeing people just out there trying to help themselves. When I was younger, I loved to hang around the older crowd, maybe I had an old soul with a baby face. I loved to hear their stories about life, the dos and don'ts. Sometimes, we would talk all night and laugh about some case scenarios. I just could not wait to all the school vacations would be out, I knew I would get back to New York and spend summer and all the school vacations and spend them with my late great-great aunt Rosie and my late uncle Leon. The best memory I had was Christmas Day. Even though my parents could not afford to buy us Christmas presents, Uncle Leon and I walked over to his friend's house, and we all just had a great time dancing and having food and laughter. These are the people who knew me before I was born. We had so much fun that presents did not even matter to me because I also had great Christmas in the past, gifts filled under the Christmas tree. Christmas is not about gifts. Like my siblings and I were poor little rich kids, but we were really poor. I knew Christmas was not about presents, but when I got older, I made a point to share what little I had with my siblings. People say the past is past, but I believe there are some lessons in the past that has an effect on the future.

I do believe that one can change the course of the past and steer it in another direction if the past was difficult. Some say forget about the past and forgive. There was one church I visited, touch on the saying forgive and forget. The Pastor said that it's okay to forgive, but you do not have to forget it. I needed to hear that especially due to the difficult childhood I had. I decided to write this, but one reason is to follow the advice I have given to some inspirational people that I just thought their road to a successful story should be heard of or told. A great educator once said that your educational goals was "people would not ask you when did you finish college, but did you finish college?" It's okay to change your goals around. Sometimes, when people get older, the dreams change. I'm going to say this again I never thought I would be writing a book; this was definitely not what I had in mind. I also work this book like an artist expressing myself, throwing my hurt and pain into words. I find the same people that I love and trusted to this very day treating me the same negative way and loved them because they are family. Sometimes, there's a thin line between friends and family. Some friends will ride harder for you than some of your very own family. Some friends or family will use you, and when they cannot benefit from you anymore, they do not have a kind word to say about you. I am only speaking from unfortunate experience. I am no stranger to writing when I was a child; my mother had these colored pens, and I would write to my cousins with these different colored pens. I did not know that writing would become my passion. After all, my English was not the best. I did well in English in high school but struggled in college with my English, and the nuns made me take eleven English classes. It was a lot of work to take those English courses. Sometimes, I would have to go catch the bus in freezing weather from my regular to another college because the English course may not be on the scheduled courses. Now that I look back, the nuns were not being hard on me; that they were just making sure I will be able to compete with the rest of the world. Now as I am writing this book, and I am coming to a close of it. I remember when I was in the sixth grade and I wrote a short story at school. I had no idea that the school was going to print it in the school newspaper. I had no idea that my hidden passion to write would become my future and current passion to write. I want this book to inspire others. Even though you feel like you are running on an invisible treadmill of life, others will notice a change in you. There is a saying I would hear in prayer meeting, "He may not come when you want him to, but he is right on time." During the lent season, some people fast by giving up something that are really a routine for them. Some people change their eating habits, others give or improve on other things in their lives.

Some of the things I have given up during the lent season help me do better and be a stronger person. I also continue with the improvement not only during the season of lent, but in everyday life. For me, I found that working a task or something to strengthen myself spiritually in life, I focus on it for a period of time. It's either something I automatically found or something that I cannot do without, and I have taken myself to another level in my life. You never know where your strengths are in life, even as a child, you do for fun, and to keep in touch with others was a sign of something in the future.

When I was a child, I love to tell stories, and I would be able to hold people's attention. Since I was raised in two different states, I would love to write my folks and family. When I was in New York, I wrote back to my folks in California; and when I was in California, I wrote back to my folks in New York. Never in a million years I did not know that it would be a hidden talent that the world would know about in the very faraway future. I would be allowed to be an assistant math teacher at the school I just had graduated from. I know no matter how hard it is in life to keep plucking away with your dreams. My dreams were unfinished; I knew that I would have to finish them. My regular paycheck cannot even make ends meet. Like the saying goes: "I am so broke I cannot even pay attention" (relaying my thoughts jokingly). I knew I had to make a great improvement in my life. I knew that my self-improvement in life would also be someone else's improvement. I have not even had the mentality of I got mine it's mine, so you on your own you just got to get yours like I struggle to get mine. Can life be so hard that a person will become an "Ebenezer Scrooge"? My story is against the odds. How is it that I can come out of such an abusive situation as a child and not to have to be on medication my whole life, and is it with all the trials and tribulation in life that I graduated at the age of seventeen years old in high school? I never met my grandparents because they passed away very tragically. My grandmother died from a home abortion, and my grandfather died from his throat closing up from the fumes working in a factory. He was also in the military. My mother was not old enough to go to school, when my grandparents had passed away. I saw the pictures of my grandmother and my grand-father; they were very good-looking couple. Grandmother was very smart, and she graduated at the age of sixteen. I know in my heart of hearts that if it was not for my great-great aunt Rosie, had not taken care of my mother, and her brother (my uncle Leon), we would had probably been orphans and maybe even had been split up as a family. I do not measure success for how many pairs of shoes I have in my closet or what kind of car I am driving or where I may reside.

I am successful in my own path and how I make an effort in try-ing to help people even more than I helped myself. When someone makes a negative statement about me that I know it may not be true, be that is their opinion and not mine. Never let a person tell you that you do not need a job that you want. No one knows you better than you. You learn to be your own critic, but do not be so hard on yourself. My other great-great aunt Gwen in California saved my life. One day, the school nurse called my home to have my mother come pick me up from school because I had a severe case of strep throat. My mother and her boyfriend came to pick me up, and at that time, we were living with relatives. She dropped me off with relatives and left back out to be with her boyfriend. I stayed in bed for three days ill and not once did my mother came home to check on me. I had not eaten in three days. My other great aunt Gwen came and told me that I had to get up and eat. She saved my life. I was about eleven years old. My thoughts are especially when I hear about a child not being treated right by their parents (whom) are all a child knows, and a mother's love and a father's love is the greatest human love a child can have, especially if you live with your parents. In the course of my life span, I became very active in church., I taught Sunday school for many years, but I truly learned myself about God and his Son Jesus Christ even more in depth. I loved the ministry of teaching service. I taught Sunday school well before I had my own family. As a child, I would be a teacher's assistant. When I was a child, I sung in the school choir; when I was an adult, I sung in the church choir. When I was a child, I love working with the elderly/seniors. When I became an adult, I joined a church missionary group where we would travel to visit the sick and the elderly. I got a couple of college degrees, not because I thought I would be financially set, but as a child, I thought in order for me to grow to think smart and be smart on how I conducted my goals and handle people, education would be the key. To my knowledge, I became the first in my family's generation to get a college degree. I am saying all this to say that there is something in your past that holds the key to your future. Staying focused is the key. I spent all my life searching for happiness. It's not easy to find, it's not going to knock at your door.

I tell people that life is only what you make it. We all know that money cannot buy you happiness, and having money is not always the answers. I have definitely learned that no matter who decided to shut me out of their lives or who never like me, they may have my respect. At least they have made it clear. So if I cut my losses, it will not be a loss at all. It just stems back to when I was a child, and I cannot understand why some of the girls at school would not accept my friendship, and my mother would tell me everyone will not like you, and so I remember what she said, and when I am an adult, I know everyone will not like me, so do not stress it out.

I learned to love myself regardless of what I have been though. I learned to look in the mirror and think I am beautiful even on my worst day. I learned the worst. I feel that I still look sharp even when I'm feeling dull. There are so many options when it comes down to your own business.

I think I have such a hard time with jobs. Even though I do well, I am not appreciated, or there were funny remarks. This must be stemmed from when I was child. The purpose of me going to college was to be able to run a business and do not have to believe

I have to work for people or a place where either I am being put down or belittled in front of people. Treating people with respect and knowing how to handle situations when you feel you do not have the authority you just cannot flip on them. Sometimes, you have to let the professional people be professional people who are also capable of making mistakes and are not owing up to them. There are lawyers, higher-ups, and sometimes they can even get hearings. Make sure if it's regarding a bill, every bill you pay, keep the receipts, put them in a large envelope or a file cabinet. Customer service people deal with thousands of people, and sometimes, accidents happen. I would get so tired of battling mentally and being so patient while dealing with professional situations, but the worst thing I could have done was to give up. It has taken me about two and a half years to complete this book. I want to let you know that people who abuse people sooner or later, the guilt catches up with them, and the truth will come out. Parents have to make sure that they are very supportive of their children and make sure they are okay, and they should not leave them for long periods of time with anyone, it doesn't matter if they are family or not. At the end of the day, they are in their parents' loving care. I had such a tough experience that my children just weren't allowed to spend time over anyone's house. Some family members I just did not allow them to go around them or be left along with due to the history of that particular family member. There's an old school song called "Pick Up the Pieces," and that's what I have done, to pick up the pieces. Sometimes, I found myself still trying to fit in where I was never wanted in the first place. There is so much out there to do. I decided to live my life the best I could and not continue to worry about why this person or that person is treating me in this manner. I live humbly, and I put God first in my life. I am not perfect nor do I claim to be. A person's character is not based on money, fame, how rich, or how poor, shy or outgoing. The human being that truly knows about the individual and what excellence a person can achieve in that individual is himself or herself. I am told that writing and English is not my thing, but I chose to do my thing. It's not based on the perception of what other people characterized me in, but the excellence I characterized myself in. I would wear a suit five days a week, and on the weekends, I wash cars and clean public restrooms, while meeting new people. There was a known department store I used to work for, I wore a dress or a skirt suit every day. I am not saying I had anything to do with the new rule, but next thing I know, the human resource officer put a new dress code into effect. All ladies are required to wear either dresses or skirts.

Every job I ever had I put a 110 percent in it. Sometimes, my coworkers would get mad, but at the end of the day, I know no matter how tough it got there, I was doing service for the Lord. I think my most daring job was chopping weeds in open fields as a teenager. I could never understand why my college friends would rather stay at home and not work at all while living off/with their family member. They just would not work or accept a job it was not what they wanted. Speaking from experience, you start doing something like I started writing books. If you say to yourself I never thought in a million years I would be doing this, think again. There may have been something in your past that you loved to do, but did not take it to another level. One of my passion and still was writing and telling attention-getting stories, and I loved singing. Learning is my passion too. You are never too old to learn. I tell people I learn something new every day. I have a picture that a former supervisor gave me when I moved on to another company, it said: "Every day is a gift."

Every day I am blessed to get up, and I make sure I get out and enjoy the air and all the time I do not have to be going anywhere particularly just getting out appreciating the gift of life. I am too busy being in competition with myself to wonder who's doing better than me and who is not. There was an old school song called "Don't Let Joneses Get You Down." I am happy for anyone who does well in life. I take no one's success that it was done with ease. Even if success and money was passed down from generation to generation in life, there is still a charge to maintain the gifts and enhance the gift that was given to you. Life is not always what you planned it to be; sometimes, you may end up going in an uphill battle, but once up, get to the top of the hill. The feeling of accomplishment is there.

Once you get to the top of the victory hill, it's much easier and faster going down the hill. The next time you go up the victory hill, it's easier, and you are better prepared than you were last time and know what obstacles were involved. There is a quote I do not know who created it, but it has a lot of truth to it that said: "Life is not a dress rehearsal." I learned if people cannot accept me for what I want to do in life and busy trying to put me down, why can they just accept me for who I am and what I want to do? One thing about walking in life you may stumble and, you may have to or may not have any humans to walk with you in life, it's okay. Sometimes, you can do better when you are alone. I always believe that man does not make my destiny. We as a human race has been given the abilities and skills to be creative and make decisions. Making goals on a weekly basis is great, because it's you who can only say I will do this for a week or a month, a fasting type of pledge; it can become a permanent fixture in your life. It's okay for me to step out of my box and comfort zone.

I started moving in a company. I was in a meeting, and the top executive was so tough. I was chiming in on the conversation, and I stood up when I talked. She kept trying in a professional manner to shut me down, but I said my comments to the conversation in a professional manner. I always had the attitude to be an example and not to be made an example. I know at the beginning of my stories I spoke about being single, I am still single, but sometimes, being alone may not be a bad thing. I come as I pleased. I do not have to check in with anyone. If I wanted to relocate, there's no discussion with my mate. I also know that there is a time and place for everything to happen. I also know there is someone for everyone who wants to be with someone. There cannot be a one-sided relationship; it really does take two.

I knew I wanted nothing more but to change my life. Once I gotten my mental health and stability back as a child, I knew I wanted a different life. I wanted to help others better their lives, though I carried a heavy load, as being the oldest child of parents that were battling their own problems, I knew I wanted better. I wanted my life to be better. I wanted my children's life to be way better than mine. Most importantly, I knew that I had three children I loved the same. I wanted my children to be close to one another. There are enough battles to deal with outside the home, so we must stick together as a family. Beating the odds is worth a try because nothing beats a failure but a try.

There were two conversations I heard from my family that I was not supposed to hear, but I did. At the age of nine years old, I got some shoes like my cousin who lived upstairs when I lived in New York. I got the shoes because we were like sisters. I did not have any sisters at the time. The shoes were two different colors my cousin did not seem to mind. Her mother was outraged she was in the kitchen talking about it, and I was in the living room. She did not know I came upstairs. Another conversation I heard was when I called my very own mother, and she was not available. I left her a voice mail, and when I checked my messages, she left me a message but did not disconnect well and called my sister and was talking about me like I was a stranger. My sister responded very nastily, "What did she want?" This is the same family that I would spend my last dime on. Sometimes, when you cannot constantly give the last dime, relationship goes out of the window. For some folks, the word family is also known as ATM machine; if the machine that cannot give you nothing at the time you go on to the next. Unfortunately, some of my friends treated me better. I chose to be something or do something different than I was accustomed to seeing.

Don't worry about people not liking you. You are who you are; you should not have to conform and dance to to everyone's tune. Like a friend once told me, "If a person does not like you, that's their problem". So, I say all this and say this again, man does not determine your destiny. If someone says something about you that you do not agree with, it does not make it true. Everyone has the right to voice their own opinion, but you don't have to agree with. No one knows you better than you. Beating the odds is a stepping stone to life's possibilities.

So the next time you are in a struggle, look at it as beating the odds is a stepping stone to your life of success. All successes do not mean money is involved, but goals are accomplished by one.

When in doubt, always remember St. Mark 10:27: "And Jesus looking upon them, saith With men it is impossible, but not with God: for with God all things are possible."

CPSIA information can be obtained
at www.ICGtesting.com
Printed in the USA
BVHW071036150419
545534BV00005B/826/P